What Your Colleagues Are Saying . . .

Discussions about improving education inevitably gravitate to things—curriculum, standards, assessments, technology, professional learning. In *The NEW School Rules*, Anthony Kim and Alexis Gonzales-Black make a highly compelling case that to fundamentally improve education we must focus on process—specifically, the organizational management, structure, and practice that governs how decisions are made. The authors provide school administrators with an accessible how-to guide for implementing the kinds of organizational changes that will lead to real improvements in student outcomes.

—JD Solomon, Editorial Director of
District Administration Magazine

When we take something as beautiful and life-giving as education, and find that managing the institutions that provide it is soul-crushing, we know something is very wrong. *The NEW School Rules* shows us the problem, offers an alternative vision of educational administration, and gives us the practical tools to unlock new energy in ourselves and our colleagues. Every administrator should read this book.

—Matthew Kramer, CEO of The Wildflower
Foundation and former co-CEO of Teach for America

The NEW School Rules offers a critical and timely framework to ensure that future generations are equipped to thrive in a rapidly changing world.

—Tony Hsieh, CEO of Zappos.com, and
New York Times bestselling author of *Delivering Happiness*

Super practical rules for school change with stated problems, lessons, and experiments you can try tomorrow. *The NEW School Rules* provides guidance on defining the work, encouraging experimentation, sharing leadership, accepting ambiguity, and turning schools into learning organizations. It is a must-read for leaders of teachers, schools, and systems.

—Tom Vander Ark, author of *Getting Smart: How Digital
Learning Is Changing the World*

Every school district should read and digest *The NEW School Rules*. In it, Anthony Kim and Alexis Gonzales-Black make a major contribution to how schools should create teams, organize, and plan to profoundly and positively impact students, teachers, and the community.

—Michael Horn, co-author of
*Disrupting Class: How Disruptive
Innovation Will Change the Way the World Learns*

The NEW School Rules is a concrete, battle-tested roadmap for leaders who want to do right by kids by having the courage to help adults embrace change. As a superintendent of ten years (in Newark and New York), I led bold teams that were relentlessly focused on turning around systems that had been failing kids for decades. The central thesis of *The NEW School Rules*—that districts and schools must fundamentally rethink how they are organized in order to become more responsive, agile, innovative and, ultimately, effective—is spot on. What I appreciate most is that the book is both visionary and evocative—and also practical and instructive. We must build education institutions that put kids' needs in an ever-evolving world ahead of everything else.

—Cami Anderson, former superintendent
of Newark Public Schools

The NEW School Rules asks the right questions and poses the right experiments to shift districts and schools to an increased focus on student learning. Kim and Gonzales-Black combine smart practices for running a great organization with the realities faced in many of America's schools. Preparing every student to succeed in the 21st century requires that educators work collaboratively to increase the quality of education.

—Tim Parker, President of NEA-Alaska

The NEW School Rules recognizes that adults in the educational system have to learn, evolve, and grow if students are to succeed in an ever-changing world. I wish I'd had this book years ago!

—Dale Erquiaga, President/CEO of
Communities in Schools and former
Nevada State Superintendent of Public Instruction

The NEW
School Rules

For my wife Angela and my mom Kay for always believing that whatever I have to say makes sense. And not to forget my dogs Bonnie (and Clyde, RIP) for being brats and teaching me to be generous.

—Anthony Kim

For Kyle and Kylan. Thank you for being my people on this long and twisty journey. All my love forever and always.

—AGB

The NEW School Rules

6 Vital Practices for Thriving and Responsive Schools

Anthony Kim and
Alexis Gonzales-Black

Illustrations by Kawai Lai

CORWIN
A SAGE Publishing Company

CORWIN
A SAGE Publishing Company

FOR INFORMATION:

Corwin

A SAGE Company

2455 Teller Road

Thousand Oaks, California 91320

(800) 233-9936

www.corwin.com

SAGE Publications Ltd.

1 Oliver's Yard

55 City Road

London EC1Y 1SP

United Kingdom

SAGE Publications India Pvt. Ltd.

B 1/I 1 Mohan Cooperative Industrial Area

Mathura Road, New Delhi 110 044

India

SAGE Publications Asia-Pacific Pte. Ltd.

3 Church Street

#10-04 Samsung Hub

Singapore 049483

Publisher: Arnis Burvikovs

Development Editor: Desirée A. Bartlett

Editorial Assistant: Eliza Riegert

Production Editor: Tori Mirsadjadi

Copy Editor: Sarah J. Duffy

Typesetter: C&M Digitals (P) Ltd.

Proofreader: Susan Schon

Indexer: Beth Nauman-Montana

Cover Designer: Alexa Turner

Marketing Manager: Nicole Franks

ISBN: 978-1-5063-5276-3

This book is printed on acid-free paper.

Certified Chain of Custody
Promoting Sustainable Forestry
www.sfiprogram.org
SFI-01268

SFI label applies to text stock

18 19 20 21 22 10 9 8 7 6 5 4 3 2

DISCLAIMER: This book may direct you to access third-party content via web links, QR codes, or other scannable technologies, which are provided for your reference by the author(s). Corwin makes no guarantee that such third-party content will be available for your use and encourages you to review the terms and conditions of such third-party content. Corwin takes no responsibility and assumes no liability for your use of any third-party content, nor does Corwin approve, sponsor, endorse, verify, or certify such third-party content.

Contents

online resources

Visit www.newschoolrules.com for additional
resources and tools created by Keara Duggan.

Preface

I've been working in the field of education, educational technology, and personalized learning for seventeen years. As the leader of several companies, I've engaged with public schools and some private ones all over the country. In just the past seven years, as founder and CEO of Education Elements, I've traveled to hundreds of states, schools, and district offices.

School districts across the country spend millions of dollars on a long list of programs and initiatives to improve student outcomes, yet we're grateful if we see student academic gains of a couple percentage points. Decisions take too long. Increasing and changing demands lead to confusion and too many things falling between the cracks. Everyone's energy is sapped in the effort to defend decisions rather than take action.

Often, we're lucky if we don't see negative results through these efforts. It's easy to point fingers at policies, the curriculum, or our people, but I've observed a different underlying issue. The culture of our schools, organizational structures, and methods of communication and decision making—not educational approaches—are the actual drivers for success or failure.

Teachers and students come to school every day, and they thrive when their school is inviting and engaging—a place where they want to be and want to spend time. District and school leaders play an important role in establishing a culture that encourages effective collaboration, creativity, and learning for everyone. Organizational practices that focus on the concept of responsiveness help schools and districts focus on the needs of the future, not the past, and rally administrators, teachers, children, families, and communities.

> *The culture of our schools, organizational structures, and methods of communication and decision making—not educational approaches—are the actual drivers for success or failure.*

That's what drove me to write this book for district and school leaders. As leadership expert Tom Northrup says, "All organizations are perfectly designed to get the results they are now getting. If we want different results, we must change the way we do things." This book is for every leader who wants to instigate change and create environments of growth, excitement, and passion.

Seeing this missing piece—improved organizational practices, not just educational ones—with the schools and educators I work with, I turned the tables on myself. How was I doing in my efforts to follow the advice and practices I was learning about and consulting on?

I decided to introduce a new set of organizational practices at Education Elements that would allow us to be faster, more responsive, and less hierarchical. In researching approaches, we decided to introduce elements of *Holacracy*®,[*] a self-management practice that increases transparency, accountability, and agility.

> *This book is for every leader who wants to instigate change and create environments of growth, excitement, and passion.*

Our team hired Alexis Gonzales-Black, my co-author, to help us. A former internal consultant on Holacracy at Zappos—the retailer that transformed the experience of buying shoes online—and founder of her own consulting firm, she is now a principal designer focused on organizational design at the firm IDEO. Alexis helped us shift to an evolving organizational structure and gave us many techniques to help move from a top-down approach to management to a new style of responsive organization based on flexible roles, shared authority, and continuous learning and change.

The more I learned about new models of leadership and organizational design, the more I saw the application to even larger systems, including the schools and districts we were working with

---

[*]Holacracy is a registered trademark of HolacracyOne, LLC.

every day. I began integrating these concepts and techniques with school leaders. The results have been tangible and effective in our own organization and in dozens of districts where we've introduced some key practices.

With evidence coming in, it was time to share what I was discovering in a book. Thus the inspiration for *The NEW School Rules* was born—an introduction to responsive, agile, and engaging organizational principles and practices applied to the world of education— and the world our students will be living and working in. I hope you'll find inspiration and practical steps to making your schools and district offices more effective, impactful, and transformative for your staff and for all the children and families you serve.

—Anthony Kim

Acknowledgments

Many people helped us bring this book to fruition. While it's impossible to highlight everyone who supported, contributed, and encouraged us in this endeavor, and gave us the space to develop it, we are indebted to all the teachers, mentors, students, thinkers, colleagues, friends, and family who have shaped our work and lives. And of course we want to share a few personal thanks.

First, we each have our current organizations to acknowledge for the insights we've gleaned working every day with such great people and the flexibility they afforded us as we faced deadlines and the large task of conceptualizing and writing a book in a field as new as organizational design for school cultures.

At Education Elements, Anthony realized that his then six-year-old organization could benefit from the new ways of organizing work he was learning about and sharing with the schools he and his teams were supporting:

> My first forays began by learning about how General Stanley McChrystal constructed a more nimble and networked Joint Special Operations Command. I collected more stories and examples, talked to people I met, and began sharing these ideas staff member by staff member, team by team, baby step by baby step. We tested and applied the concepts we came to see as responsive organizational practices. The following people really worked hard to steer the organization into implementing these practices: Jenni Tonti, Amy Jenkins, Justin DeLeon, Ben Politzer, Filip Kesler, Will Cody, and Jennifer Kirchner.

Alexis would not have discovered her passion for organizational design and change if Zappos hadn't given her the chance to follow her passion across the company:

> I have never forgotten Christa Foley's words when I proposed leaving the Learning and Development team and moving to the newly formed Holacracy team. Christa said, "I want you to stay in your current role, but one of our core values is Pursue Growth and Learning, and it wouldn't be in line with our values if I didn't support you to go." To Christa, John, Hollie, Tony, Beverly, Alicia, Celina, and all the Zapponians who provided mentorship and modeled what it meant to live true to core values, I owe you an incredible debt of gratitude.

As we emphasize in the book, Alexis's early growth as an organizational design practitioner was inspired by the practice of Holacracy. Alexis thanks Brian, Oliver, Karilen, and all the Holacracy One coaches and extended network that provided partnership and feedback, which strengthened her practice. She also values her community at Responsive Org:

> To the visionary leaders of Responsive Org who graciously invited me to contribute and stand alongside them in this wonderful thriving community, thank you. Specific thanks to Mike Arauz, Adam Pisoni and Aaron Dignan for being my first co-conspirators. I also want to thank my private consulting business partner and friend John Bunch. No one has had more of a singular impact on my career than you. From the Holacracy team to Thoughtful Org, and hopefully many more adventures. Thank you.

Together, we were inspired by many people who shared their academic and research experiences, lessons learned, and challenges, which helped us think through and test the principles, practices, and recommendations we present.

A number of colleagues and friends helped shape our ideas in crucial ways, including Thoughtful Org client organizations and partners, and the organizational design team at IDEO. Thanks also to friends that shared their early feedback on the book: Katie Hill, Seth Rau, Allison Serafin, Aliy Bossert, and Kyle Wendel, who were so responsive and generous with their time.

We are especially grateful to Kawai Lai, who saved us at the last minute with the wonderful illustrations in the book. We would also like to thank Keara Duggan for creating tools related to the experiments in the book. A special acknowledgment goes to Janet Goldstein, a gifted collaborator who helped us hone our ideas, shaped our writing, and made this process easier and our ideas flow into something everyone can understand and appreciate. Our publishing team at Corwin has supported us with their initial enthusiasm and their care for the book every step of the way.

Alexis wants to thank Anthony, first for giving her a shot at transforming Education Elements and then believing in this work enough to partner on this book. Thank you for the structure and patience as I worked through a new job, new baby, and all of life's plot twists over the past year and a half. Mom and Dad, Deborah and Don, thank you for shaping my first examples of what hard work and commitment look like and thank you for your unconditional love and for always encouraging me to pursue my dreams. To my brother Jacob, thank you for your humor and friendship that keep me grounded. Finally, to my partner Kyle Wendel for putting up with my crazy work and writing schedule, and for your attention and love that make me feel like I can do anything in the world.

Anthony expresses thanks to everyone at Education Elements for being open to experimenting with these new concepts that helped him formulate and refine some of the concepts in the book. To Alexis who guided me through my learning of these practices, who always surprises me with how deep her knowledge and understanding is for responsive organizational design. Her ability to make these practices almost simple helped me transfer these tools to education. To my mother, who unconditionally believes that I can do anything I set my mind to. And most lovingly, thanks to my wife Angela, who let me be selfish and gave up our weekends and evenings so I could write this book and train for my triathlons.

Publisher's Acknowledgments

Corwin gratefully acknowledges the contributions of the following reviewers:

Kathy Rhodes, Principal
Hinton Elementary
Hinton, IA

Melissa Wood-Glusac, English Teacher Grades 9 and 11
Thousand Oaks High School
Thousand Oaks, CA

Dr. Jill Gildea, Superintendent
Greenwich Public Schools
Greenwich, CT

Nicky Kemp, Assistant Superintendent
North Callaway R-1 School District
Kingdom City, MO

Rick Yee, Principal
McAuliffe School
Saratoga, CA

About the Authors

Anthony Kim is a nationally recognized leader in education technology, school design, and personalized learning. As founder and CEO of Education Elements, he has been involved in helping hundreds of schools change the way they think about teaching and learning. As the author of *Personalized Learning Playbook: Why the Time Is Now*, Anthony has influenced many educators. He has contributed to many publications on new school models, including *Lessons Learned From Blended Programs: Experiences and Recommendations From the Field*. Anthony is a nationally recognized speaker on personalized learning, and his work has been referenced by the Christensen Institute, iNACOL, EdSurge, CompetencyWorks, *Education Week, District Administrator,* and numerous other research reports.

Anthony also founded Provost Systems, which provided online learning solutions to school districts. Provost Systems was acquired by EdisonLearning, where he served as executive vice president of online. Anthony is passionate about helping school districts become more nimble, understanding what motivates adult learners, and designing schools that plan for the needs of our future.

Outside of education, Anthony is passionate about triathlons and learning about people who overcome remarkable challenges. He is a San Francisco native and continues to live there with his wife Angela and rescued dogs.

Alexis Gonzales-Black is an expert in organizational design and change initiatives with deep experience in the education, retail, and technology sectors. A principal designer at the global design firm IDEO, she designs and implements new organizational models to fuel innovation, agility, and engagement.

Alexis earned a BS in biology from James Madison University and developed a passion for teaching and social justice as a high school science teacher and recruitment director for Teach for America. At Zappos, Alexis led college recruiting and diversity initiatives before co-leading the online retailer's transition to the Holacracy model of organizational design. She founded Thoughtful Org Partners, a consultancy where she partners with organizations to break through rigidity and introduce self-organizing principles and practices.

Alexis's work has been widely covered in such media outlets as *Forbes, Huffington Post,* Fox, and CNN Money. She is a board member of Responsive Org and formerly a member of the Nevada State Board of Education and the WestEd Board of Directors. She lives in the San Francisco Bay Area with her family.

Introduction

WHY WE NEED NEW ORGANIZATIONAL PRACTICES FOR THRIVING SCHOOLS AND STUDENTS TODAY

In all the discussion about schools and school reform, most educational communities—and all the political, philanthropic, and public communities—have their attention focused on what is being taught and the methods being used to teach it. Comparatively little time is being spent on how schools themselves are organized and run to do this work or on the differences in how small and large schools, charter schools, and alternative schools do things.

All this is to say, little attention is being paid to the underlying organizational, management, and work practices in the field of education. Yet we've discovered something powerful in our hands-on work with organizations and schools of all types: *If we don't change how schools work and how they are organized, we won't ever realize the full potential of the work they do.* Counterintuitively, not only does time spent on understanding how schools and districts work help resolve internal dysfunctions, it also leads to more time spent on educational content and pedagogy, and more energy for students and classroom learning.

Today's school management and leadership practices still follow a model that was developed for educational success in the early 20th century. The model was designed to prepare a narrower and much less diverse group of students for their futures in highly structured environments—the factory and the large organization.

> *If we don't change how schools work and how they are organized, we won't ever realize the full potential of the work they do.*

The world has changed. The ways of working are changing, and our students have certainly changed. Yet our schools have been isolated from the seismic shifts happening in the new world of work. Our educational organizations have been largely cut off from, and lack experience with, changes occurring in the corporate and startup worlds. Schools have been left behind. Too often they get stuck in routine ways of doing things, and when they want to do something new, they can be met with lots of fear, negativity, frustration, and resistance.

Here some of the realities schools are facing:

- With the increased acceptance of technology in school districts, schools are struggling to keep up with the constant platform changes, issues with data privacy, and shifts in expectations. While most people use technology seamlessly and pervasively in their personal lives, there are a lot of conflicting ideas about the "proper" role of technology in the classroom, as if classrooms are fundamentally different from the workplace and the home.

- Teacher recruitment and retention has become a nationwide challenge. The cohorts of younger teachers want to know they are being heard and have an impact every day. They are looking for opportunities to make a difference beyond the classroom. We need to empower districts, schools, and even teachers to become designers of learning experiences.

- It's always been incredibly difficult for district leaders—and, as a result, school-level leaders—to shift priorities due to the impact any change will have on their budgets. Funding streams are often unreliable, which means attention to new issues and problems is often inconsistent. Unintentionally, the budget can seem more important than the people—teachers and students— when decisions are made to eliminate some initiatives or change people and assignments to meet these challenges.

To stay competitive, and to simply seize opportunities, businesses today are reinventing how they work and embracing responsiveness to create cultures of engagement and organizational models of continuous innovation, learning, and change. Our schools need to do the same—not only to function better, but to prepare students for the world they will be entering. Schools can't stop the speed of new ideas and opportunities, but they can incorporate more nimble ways of working that make change and experimenting part of the culture of schools and learning. And when they do, there's no going back—the vibrancy and excitement and impact is too great.

The Promise of Responsiveness

We've discovered in our hands-on work with schools all over the country that the schools that *are* working—and there are many—always create, early on, environments designed for evolution, responsiveness, and continuous learning. This is our thesis and the purpose of this book. A new approach to the management, organizational practices, and work of schools is an essential component to the success of students in our schools.

> Schools that are working—and there are many—always create, early on, environments designed for evolution, responsiveness, continuous learning. This is our thesis and the purpose of this book.

A *responsive organization*, as we use the term, is one that puts responsiveness at its foundation—responsiveness to new information; to the needs and talents of staff, teachers, students, and the community; to unforeseen challenges and opportunities. Responsive schools and districts embrace

- an iterative and evolving approach to planning and structure,

- meaningful autonomy for teams and team members,

- approaches to sharing and receiving information and feedback that build trust and engagement and allow for timely and effective decision making.

A responsive organizational approach has three big promises that can also serve as a guide to measure success. Schools and districts that are designed for responsiveness, evolution, and continuous learning demonstrate these hallmarks:

1. *Responsive schools and districts are alive and changing.* Like living organisms, responsive schools and districts are continuously evolving in response to real-world conditions. Teams, and the projects they work on, evolve to better achieve their outcomes, even when that change is hard or disruptive. As teachers, supervisors, principals, and district staff and leaders embrace change, they experience new levels of engagement and excitement. This dynamism becomes a magnet to attract great talent, students, and community partners.

2. *Responsive schools and districts have a clear and motivating purpose.* Everyone understands and shares the larger mission, the purpose of specific initiatives they are working toward, and the part they play as individuals serving that mission—and this spreads all the way to the classroom.

3. *Responsive schools and districts are continuously acting, evolving, improving, and aiming higher.* Adults and students are engaged in learning, growing in multiple ways, taking action, trying and failing, and reaching for new goals that might be organizational, technical, personal, or even emotional. Students, teachers, and staff are all involved in a learning community that also includes the broader community of families and towns.

What we're describing and advocating for is an organic, alive, growing model for schools, not a fixed one borrowed from the industrial age that sought predictability and uniformity. (Work that is "uniform" is being replaced by technology, computers, and robots.) We're looking at schools and organizations as organic structures made up of people, who are organic as well. In organic environments, processes that aren't working die off and those that are working thrive and continue to evolve and spread.

This needed shift to organic, responsive schools speaks to the truth everyone wants to ignore. Across the board, but especially with today's new generation of teachers, educators are turned off by the pressure and lack of rewards. They want more flexibility, more recognition, and more sense of being part of schools that matter.

We don't have to wait for permission or some new program rollout. We can begin to create environments where our schools and districts are alive, have purpose, and are continuously learning and growing.

How Responsive Organizational Thinking Evolved

From the publication of *The Principles of Scientific Management* by Frederick Taylor during the height of the industrial age to the seminal texts of Peter Drucker, considered the father of modern management, to today's emerging management theories, there has always been thinking and practice around improving the outcomes of our organizations.

The field of organizational design, which began to take hold in the late 1980s and 1990s, follows in the footsteps of management theory but asks a broader question: Instead of asking, "How can our managers influence better performance?" the practice of organizational design asks, "What levers of influence—from strategy, structure, and processes to tools and talent—can be designed to influence certain behaviors and outcomes?"

> We don't have to wait for permission or some new program rollout. We can begin to create environments where our schools and districts are alive, have purpose, and are continuously learning and growing.

Responsive organizational design encompasses one cutting-edge approach to organizational design that is focused on how organizations can deal with complexity and speed in rapidly changing environments. You can see examples of responsive organizational design in theories and practices from many approaches—from the ecological management practices of Native Americans (Anderson, 2013) to more recently applied business cases like Zappos's adoption of Holacracy (Greenfield, 2015) or the self-management practice of tomato-processing company Morning Star (Hamel, 2011). These approaches, along with other innovative designs for organizations, are rapidly being adopted and studied. A collective of thought leaders in the field created a manifesto for responsive organizations, which they define as "built to learn and respond rapidly through the open flow of information; encouraging experimentation and learning on rapid cycles; and organizing as a network of employees, customers, and partners motivated by shared purpose" (Responsive.org, n.d., para. 4).

Some of the language on responsive organizational design we use in this book may echo approaches from James Spillane (2006), Steve Zuieback (2012), and Michael Fullan (2004), whose work focuses on responsive leadership. *The NEW School Rules* is not about leadership practices per se. Rather, we are describing ground rules for an organization to function at the pace of the world around us. Our perspective is influenced by our experiences with the self-management practice of Holacracy (Robertson, 2015), pioneered by consulting company Holacracy One, and teal organizations, as outlined by Frederic Laloux (2014) in his book *Reinventing Organizations*. Both of these organizational approaches are notable for their disciplined guidance on methods and concrete techniques that engender responsive cultures.

The approach to responsive organizations we're presenting in this book can be thought of as an operating system for responsive schools and school districts. The ideas we present here are based on the belief that static and rigid organizational systems no longer work—whether the organization is a huge corporation, a startup, a school district, or a school team, information is traveling too fast and the rate of change is quicker and more unpredictable than ever before. Schools that are responsive to the changing conditions around them can better respond to the educational needs of their students while modeling for students the world they are being prepared for.

> The approach to responsive organizations we're presenting in this book can be thought of as an operating system for responsive schools and school districts. . . . Schools that are responsive to the changing conditions around them can better respond to the educational needs of their students.

How This Book Is Designed

In *The NEW School Rules*, we look at responsive practices in six domains of school organizations today. For each domain we provide one New Rule and a set of principles and practices that can be adapted to school organizations of different scales, communities, and cultures. These New Rules work together as building blocks. Of course, they are presented sequentially, but they are parts of a whole. As you progress through each of the domains, you'll see how they work together to create more responsive cultures and organizations—and effective schools.

Here are the six domains we'll be exploring:

1. **Planning**—how to find the right purpose and plan to achieve it

2. Teaming—what makes teams function as powerful, effective groups that lead projects and change

3. Managing Roles—new ways of thinking about who should do the work to unleash expertise, interest, and desire to learn

4. Decision Making—the truth about who gets to decide and how a new model of decision making can speed up experimentation, change, and engagement

5. Sharing Information—the nuance of putting out information and actual communication that leads to a powerful shared purpose

6. The Learning Organization—coming full circle, the importance of school organizations that have a learning culture to model and test the learning culture we want and need for our students

Each chapter is structured for ease of reading and later reference, with the following sections included for each of the six domains:

- *The Problem*: A snapshot of what isn't working anymore and why. We look at why change is needed, with examples and touchstones. This is the part of the chapter where readers nod their heads—and possibly groan—in agreement.

- *The New Rule*: What we propose as an alternate, responsive principle along with a working thesis for overcoming the problem. The New Rules are phrased as familiar sayings and can be used as shared mantras. When a group gets stuck, the New Rules can provide simple starting points. Even if you don't remember all the details of a chapter, you can remember the six New Rules in *The NEW School Rules* and the concepts that underlie them.

- *Case Study*: Each chapter includes one longer case study from our work with a wide range of schools and districts around the country. The ideas and challenges they illustrate occur in all types of schools and every size district, from the tiniest to the biggest metropolitan areas with thousands of staff and hundreds of schools. These case studies are not comprehensive, but there is a reason to provide the highlights and not the entire plan. As you'll see in Chapter 1, you can learn from others, but you can't repeat someone else's solution.

Responsiveness means learning and adapting to one's own environment and ever-changing conditions.

- *Lessons*: To make the book as accessible and inspirational as possible, we've identified two to four lessons, or practices, that break the New Rule down into actionable concepts. They illustrate lessons from the case study and show ways the New Rule can be understood and applied incrementally. Keep in mind that the concepts and mindsets presented in the lessons are more important than any specific detail. We encourage you to capture the *aha* moments and transfer them to your circumstances.

- *Experiments*: Each chapter ends with a set of two to four experiments for you and your colleagues to try. We chose to call them *experiments* rather than *implementation steps* or *best practices* because an experiment begins with a hypothesis. The experiments we share in each chapter come from our hypotheses related to creating responsive school organizations. They are based on our years of observations, direct work in schools, and research in organizational design. These experiments may or may not work as is or in an adapted form. Try them. Identify what's working and what's not, and evolve these strategies over time. Happy experimenting!

- *It's working when . . .*: A summary at the end of each chapter of key takeaways for each New Rule.

- *Business stories*: The worlds of school and work have become too cut off from each other. We share stories of well-known organizations from Wal-Mart to the U.S. Army to Starbucks to show how they have used aspects of responsive organizations to further their missions. These stories are not intended as literal examples to be followed in our classrooms and offices, but as lightbulbs of possibilities.

- *Call-out quotes*: This is not a workbook or a how-to manual, but we do provide real advice with real applications. Along with the summary lists and "It's working when . . ." sections, the call-out quotes featured throughout the book highlight key learnings and takeaways. Of course, we encourage you to highlight the ideas and examples that speak to you and your situation most directly.

The book concludes with the following sections:

- *A Responsive Roadmap*: This presents a five-step sequence for getting started, experiments to try, ways to go deeper, and how to evaluate progress.

- *Frequently Asked Questions*: You may find yourself saying, "Yes, but . . ." or "I only wish we could . . . ." The answers we provide in this list will make the most sense once you've absorbed the principles and lessons in the book, but you'll get some reassurance and inspiration if you read these notes as you go along.

- *List of New Rules and Lessons and List of Experiments*: As an easy reference, we've included lists of the New Rules, Lessons, and Experiments. You might make a copy of these lists or have them on an accessible platform as a handy cheat sheet for you and your team members.

A Note About Who This Book Is For

Whether you are a teacher, professional learning community leader, school administrator, superintendent, or playing any other crucial role in the education system, you can use the New Rules, lessons, and experiments in this book to get started in your area and with your immediate colleagues.

If you are a superintendent or another leader seeking new ways of evolving your school or district and culture, this book will provide you with many entry points and is a great resource to share with anyone and everyone who raises their hand to be a leader of responsiveness in your schools and district. (Refer to the Roadmap and Frequently Asked Questions at the back of the book to get started.)

No matter what your starting point, all you need in order to become more responsive is this book and a healthy dose of curiosity.

* * *

We hope this book will be an exciting journey. We want to share principles we've implemented that help districts and other organizations thrive. We want to give you a new way of looking at the work you do and how you do it. We want to share techniques and how-tos to get you started easily tomorrow and some approaches that are more advanced to add over time. Ultimately, we want to inspire you to see that change is possible, exciting, and part of learning. It's not something to avoid but something to embrace.

The 21st century demands a whole new understanding of change. It's no longer occasional or optional. If we get comfortable with change and the doors it opens, and learn the skills and principles to harness it, we will have done something powerful for our students, our communities, and ourselves. Things that seemed impossible become possible.

CHAPTER 1

Planning

Plan for Change, Not Perfection

U.S. general and president Dwight Eisenhower said, "In preparing for battle, I have always found that plans are useless, but planning is indispensable."

If "better student outcomes" is our shared mantra as educators, then we need to stick vigilantly to that purpose as our guiding principle and direction, not the plans we make to get us there. We don't want to be sidelined by our strategies, action steps, and rubrics, which can often take on lives of their own. We need to approach planning as a way of thinking, not a set product or plan that has value in and of itself. We need our planning to inspire, lead, and unify our organizations, teams, and teachers. Otherwise, we can achieve the plan but not the purpose we set out to achieve.

The Problem

Imagine you are the district leader who, under pressure to implement a one-to-one technology initiative, ordered brand-new tablets for 10,000 students. You carefully determined your needs and managed to come just under the budget for the initiative. However, there was a problem. You hadn't factored in the cost of software to run on the devices. You assumed they would just work.

> *We need our planning to inspire, lead, and unify our organizations, teams, and teachers. Otherwise, we can achieve the plan but not the purpose we set out to achieve.*

Once you realized you needed funds to purchase additional software, what did you do? Did you move ahead with the one-to-one initiative and hope that free software would suffice? Or did you reduce the number of devices you ordered so you could allocate funds for the software?

This really happened—in lots of places. It turns out many districts opted for the former. They deployed the devices across their schools so they could "check the box" and execute the plan—no matter how limited the utility of the devices.

While we try to make the best plans possible, as quickly as possible, the question is: How can any organization execute a plan with constantly changing variables?

WHEN PLANS ARE MORE IMPORTANT THAN OUR PURPOSE

All of us have been expected to put together a strategic plan, whether it's for one semester or 5 years. We labor over these plans—sometimes over the course of 12 to 24 months—dreaming up the path ahead and detailing the resources we'll need. We aim to be future focused, but out of necessity our assumptions are based on the current realities of our schools and districts. Then we present our plan for approval.

Unfortunately, once we're set to go, we find the situation has changed before we've gotten started. Technology programs or platforms may have changed or been discontinued. People have changed—in districts with a high number of students receiving free or reduced-price lunch, teacher turnover can be over 22 percent (Di Carlo, 2015)—and the new team isn't up to speed. Policies have evolved and buy-in has dropped off. Yet many of us have been penalized when we don't follow the plan. We can't seem to let go of this pattern, repeating the process year after year.

The plan offers a comforting illusion. It suggests we can anticipate the future and prevent failures, but ultimately it is only an illusion. Your mind may automatically default to the old adage "If you fail to plan, you plan to fail." But try this thought experiment:

Is failure occurring in your organization?

Are you falling short of goals, missing benchmarks, or experiencing any degree of failure already?

The answer is probably yes.

Failure, at least to some degree, is inevitable. In fact, by failing early and often we can limit the negative impact of failure and benefit from the experience and data we gain in the process. Failure helps us surface organizational deficiencies and uncover our own blind spots. And of course it gives us a good dose of humility. It's hard to imagine that anyone has the capability of planning perfectly, anticipating every action. In fact, it could be argued that the most successful organizations are able to execute in parallel with failures.

Take school improvement planning as an example. Generally, low-performing schools are compelled to create a cumbersome plan outlining goals, actions, benchmarks, evaluations, and more. The length and complexity of these plans almost ensures that no one understands how they should be used, and they are often developed by people far removed from the day-to-day work and the real needs on the ground. Planning in a vacuum ties teams and schools to a plan, emotionally and mentally, to everyone's detriment. It makes it harder to adapt, even when data—and the larger purpose—suggest taking a different route.

> *Planning in a vacuum ties teams and schools to a plan, emotionally and mentally, to everyone's detriment. It makes it harder to adapt, even when data and the larger purpose—suggest taking a different route.*

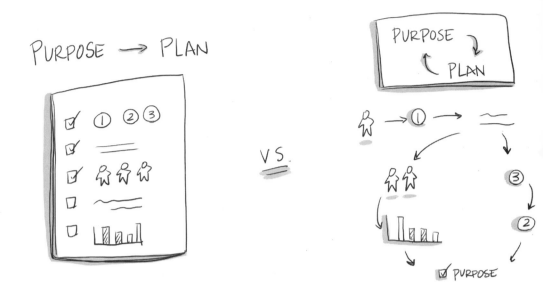

PLANNING WITHOUT LEARNING

Planning is often a way for organizations to cope with uncertainty. A plan makes things feel more concrete and knowable, but it also creates a false sense of security. For example:

- Imagine a plan that focuses on making sure there is bandwidth at schools. What if after you execute this plan, which was done flawlessly, you realize that there is not enough bandwidth for the types of applications the schools end up using? Even though the plan and support systems were executed well, was the project a success? What was the purpose of the plan? To expand Internet access or to create new learning opportunities and strategies?

- Many districts are looking for a silver bullet to address the needs of low-performing students. Districts that look at programs like Multi-Tiered Systems of Support (MTSS) develop complex implementation plans and procedures to follow. However, the districts are not learning as they are implementing because these types of prescriptive programs are often rigidly designed and difficult to adapt to individual schools and students.

- As districts roll out new curriculum adoptions, they continue to spend inordinate amounts of time mapping standards. Sometimes it can take years to unpack standards across all grade levels and subjects. By the time they are done, the district teams are exhausted, the project is delayed, and there are no vendors that can meet all of the requirements.

In trying to find a reason for falling short of goals, we attribute the lack of results to not executing the plan well enough. We insist that if only we had a more robust plan, or stuck closer to the plan, we would have succeeded. This is where we get caught in a cycle of creating more and more detailed plans every year.

> *In trying to find a reason for falling short of goals, we attribute the lack of results to not executing the plan well enough.*

When our plans are not designed to account for learning as we go, we ignore emerging information and clues like common sense and logic. It can lead to the opposite of what was hoped for—plans sitting on the shelf, half-hearted implementation, and skepticism carried over to the next initiative that comes along. I've heard this time and time again about strategic plans and strategic plan refreshes. Kind of like Groundhog Day—you dust off the old one and start a refresh every few years, with very little of the old one implemented.

CONTROL IS CONFUSED WITH PLANNING

Plans become more important than the purpose when control is confused with planning. As an example, this frequently happens with learning management systems. The system may be designed to provide personalized skills training and professional development for teachers, but administrators frequently default to using it as a tool to monitor performance by tracking teacher logins. The original planning may focus on teacher development, but the plan may focus on measurements and can feel punitive. Even though you can collect data on teacher task and usage, how can you tell if teachers were willing to learn, learned, or are applying what they learned? Is it good enough just to track whether teachers did the work?

In the 1880s, Frederick Taylor came up with a style of management, which peaked in influence in the 1910s and 1920s, though many practices continue to this day. His approach to management was scientific and based on efficiency, especially labor productivity, standardized practices, and the transformation of craft into mass production. This approach aimed to reduce workers to replaceable parts—which would eventually be mechanized and automated—resulting in a greater division of labor and a lost connection to the production of the products. The purpose was to eliminate any deviations in order to produce a consistent product. Workers began to feel their labor was monotonous and lacked meaning, and it was often exploited, leading to a rise of united workers and unions.

The creativity, responsiveness, and learning that naturally came with the work of the craftsperson or small business owner was "planned out" of the industrial model of work. The role of the teacher in many ways has been reduced to a set of repetitive routines. The focus on accountability, pacing guides, and standards has whittled away the creative side of teaching. Our mental model of planning in schools still comes from this 19th and 20th century picture of workers. However, the creative element is what makes learning exciting and motivating for teachers and students. Yet there's a way to have both—accountability and creative responsiveness.

The New Rule

Plan for Change, Not Perfection

To think about planning that is responsive, adaptable, and amazingly sophisticated, we can look to nature for inspiration. Take, for example, a human cell. We can think of genetic code, or genes, as a blueprint containing instructions to build hundreds of millions of different components for the body. Rather than execute the blueprint identically in every cell, the body can turn certain genes on and off to trigger specific developmental pathways, adapt to new food sources, or cope with environmental stresses. The versatility and adaptability of our genes allows our bodies to respond and thrive under various conditions.

How can we design systems in human organizations that have the necessary building blocks without creating rigidity based on fixed rules, uniformity, and control? How can we allow for flexibility and adaptability so our planning serves us rather than limits us?

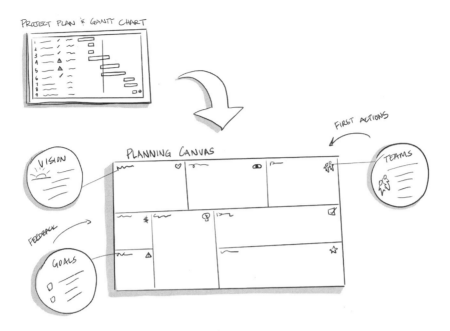

The goal of planning is to get directional clarity so people know where to focus their attention and how to make sense of situations as they come about. If we begin to *plan for change, not perfection,* we continually stay open to new, better, and different options we may discover along the way.

This New Rule follows an approach of *planning and iterating* rather than the traditional one of *planning and control,* which focuses on compliance. This new approach gives us permission to change the plan when overwhelming data suggest a change of course. It sets the stage for a feedback process in which actions are continuously shaped by and adapted to changing conditions (such as feedback from parents, from teachers, from students) rather than by a master plan established at the beginning of the year—or the year before that!

> How can we allow for flexibility and adaptability so our planning serves us rather than limits us?

Simon Sinek (2009), in his book *Start With Why,* states that every organization functions on three levels: what we do, how we do it, and why we do it (pp. 37–51). He proposes that while most people focus on the *how* and *what,* great leaders focus on the *why.* He defines the *why* as the larger purpose, cause, or belief—it's the answer to the question of why we get up in the morning or why the work we do should matter to anyone else.

Clarity of purpose gives you permission to evolve and make changes to the plan, as long as they are in service to the greater mission.

> A new approach to planning gives us permission to change the plan when overwhelming data suggest a change of course.

At Inditex, the parent company of fast fashion retailer Zara, the purpose is simple: Keep the customer at the center of everything the company does. It's this laser focus and a *plan and iterate* approach to planning that has allowed Zara to develop some of the most innovative business models in the world. Rather than manufacturing huge orders of a certain item, Zara manufactures in small batches, sends merchandise to stores, receives data, and then doubles down on the styles that are successful. The company invests heavily in the flow of information to gather sales and trend information. Then it acts on the data with a production process that allows it to get new styles and more inventory into stores in just 2 weeks, rather than the customary 6 months of its competitors. Zara invests its time and marketing dollars in responsiveness rather than selling with advertising and high-paid celebrities (Hanson, 2012). This approach has made it a global leader in its industry.

Wal-Mart does this too, with intensive morning meetings where managers share the sales and revenue results of product displays that are working in one location so they can be replicated across regions or the whole country in a matter of hours. Every day is an experiment in using data for feedback and responsiveness (PBS, 2004).

In a school setting, principals do this regularly at the start of a school year. Over the spring and summer, the school tries to predict the enrollment by grade level to plan for classrooms, bus schedules, and teaching staff. However, the predictions are regularly off and schools scramble to add staff, move classrooms, and redesign the bell schedule. They make plans, but ideally they anticipate and are prepared for change. A school that has a flex day schedule is able to adjust to its Plan Z schedule (such as periods that are 10 minutes shorter) to fit in special events, guest speakers, and workshops that weren't on the schedule in August.

The differences in these two strategies are summed up in the following table:

Comparison of Planning Approaches

Plan and Control	Plan and Iterate
Develop the plan, gain support for it, then execute it.	Develop the plan, execute it, then rework or redesign it based on feedback.
The plan is driven by past behaviors and information.	The plan is driven by real-time observations and data.
Build plans that are extremely detailed and as close to perfect as possible.	Build plans that are good enough for now, recognizing that more information and learning are to come.
Stick to the plan in order to measure the success of the plan.	Adapt the plan to support purpose in order to measure the success of the plan.

Think about the time, money, and resources you could save if you and your team and colleagues adopted the rule of *plan for change, not perfection*.

....

CASE STUDY

Case Study: When a Large District Plans for Change

A southeastern county school district is rapidly growing, with about 100,000 students and close to 100 schools. It's a noncontiguous district serving the areas outside a large city. The School Board in 2011 hired Raymond to replace the existing superintendent. Raymond's first moves were to develop a new strategic plan around personalized learning and to make the district a charter district. By 2013, the district had developed its roadmap, which included a rollout of new technology, school designs, and professional development to 100 schools in twelve to eighteen months.

Led by the then deputy superintendent of academics, Sean, a team was pulled together that included the formation of a Frontline Team, made up of district-level coaches who focus on transformative practices, technology skills, and applied learning.

The initiative got started in 2012 with an initial effort to scan for "bright spots" in K–12 schools across the state. What they found was that schools that were student-centered could help them achieve the goals they had identified:

- 90 percent of students graduating on time

- 80 percent of seniors competitive for admissions to the state university system

- 100 percent of students career ready

To make the transition to student-centered learning, the district's leadership team envisioned classrooms at every level would move along a continuum from traditional learning to personalized learning. Teachers and students would start simply with technology used as a tool to enhance learning. Over time, the schools would move all the way to a competency-based framework where students would have choice around their assignments and pace of learning.

Everyone realized it would be impossible to align 10,500 employees around a detailed project plan of this scale. If the plan got too complex and detailed, it would be hard for people feel a sense of ownership, and more time would be spent explaining the details of the plan than actually working on it. They decided to take a dramatically different approach to the usual strategic plan:

- They would create a flexible approach for teachers with a "start where you're comfortable" and "progress at your own rate" design.

- They would focus on telling a story to inspire excitement and shared understanding.

- They would measure progress and growth.

They figured the more excited and knowledgeable people were about the plan, the more readily they would adopt it. This insight affected the planning itself. They realized they could expend enormous amounts of time trying to map out all the details and contingencies without having enough experience to do it effectively. They also sensed it would overwhelm the very people they needed to get on board.

The solution they came up with was to devise a roadmap showing the reality of where the districts was, what success would look like, and key elements of the path they would take to get there. It would allow plenty of room for adaptation and change as the implementation got underway. Letting go of the notion of the perfect plan created a situation where they felt they could get a reasonable plan together in a short time frame, which they could refine as they learned from their initial assumptions and the actual experiences of students and teachers.

The roadmap comprised these key features:

- *Their future state:* Schools provide differentiated and individualized learning to all students through student-centered learning models, flexible and project-driven learning, integrated assessments, and school autonomy.

- *Their current state:* Schools needed more professional development; they lacked an integrated technology plan; a strong decision-making framework needed to be implemented to move quickly.

- *The path they wanted to follow:* Key streams of work for the next five years across the curriculum were identified as learning, tools and resources, and operations.

- *The near term actions they needed to take to align working groups:* The project team would provide schools with a clear vision, frequent communications, and ways to collect feedback for continuous improvement.

- *How success would be measured:* Processes to collect and interpret qualitative and quantitative data needed to be in place at the outset in order to support ongoing iteration with real information and feedback.

To make the concept of student-centered learning less abstract, the roll-out of the roadmap included the story of a hypothetical student named Monica. For example, 11-year-old Monica would use her personal dashboard on a tablet throughout her day. She could be reminded of something a teacher said in class by watching videos of lectures. Every day, data would be recorded about Monica's coursework and progress, which would become part of her online profile. Her teacher would diagnose and recommend resources and communicate with Monica's parents based on that information.

Monica's story brought to life the central idea of co-planning between students, teachers, and parents. It emphasized how students would participate in and demonstrate their learning and would be engaged by choice and variable learning environments to define their learning paths based on career- and college-readiness standards.

The storytelling approach to planning was also applied to the evaluation aspect of the plan. They wanted to come up with a simple purpose, or goal, for each year of the initiative. It needed to be specific enough to be measurable and broad enough to allow for flexibility and varying needs across so many different schools, teachers, and students.

THE SCHOOL DISTRICT'S PLANNING FOR SUCCESS

Success was defined as follows:

Year 1	
Goal:	Instructional practice is changing and students are more engaged.
Measured by:	Teacher surveys, classroom observations, review of digital content usage data
Year 2	
Goal:	Instructional strategies are positively impacting student performance and engagement.

Measured by: Formative benchmarks and state assessments, student retention

Year 3 and Beyond

They didn't plan the later years because they didn't have data from Year 1 to inform their plans. Once they got to Year 2 they would develop new plans to continue their implementation work.

For every school in the county, the aim was to make progress. There was a wide range of classroom designs to achieve more student-centered, personalized learning, ranging from very simple models to highly complex ones that fit the abilities of the most proficient and experienced teachers. As long as teachers were progressing on the roadmap, they had the go-ahead and autonomy to continue at their pace.

The new strategic plan basically established a five-year continuum for teachers to move from a traditional learning model to a personalized, student-centered learning model. There wouldn't be a standard, one-size-fits-all pace for implementation. Rather, teachers were allowed to select a level they were comfortable with and then progress to the next level. This allowed teachers who preferred a more cautious approach to avoid taking a massive leap, which might result in them falling on their face. This progression model increased autonomy and creativity and motivated teachers to learn, participate, and engage in the work.

In 2015, Raymond and Sean moved on to new senior leadership roles in other districts. With a change in leadership, many school districts drop or curtail current initiatives, since they may be complex and hard to understand and embrace, and they start on a brand new strategic plan. However, we believe the roadmap approach allowed new people to shape the effort as it evolved. It seemed that broad ownership of the work throughout the district continued to move the original vision forward. All one hundred schools in the county have adopted new school designs aligned to the district vision, guided by the roadmap and their continuous improvement process.

Lessons

We believe that the success the school district in the case study experienced relied on everyone's willingness to eschew the traditional model of detailed strategic planning. Instead they painted a clear picture of the future state and asked people to come along with them on a journey in an environment that supported teachers to take iterative steps and learn along the way.

There are several key lessons about iterative planning we can cull from their success:

- Build roadmaps, not manuals.

- Use cadences and pivot points, not just schedules and deadlines.

- Encourage testing, experiments, and responsiveness.

BUILD ROADMAPS, NOT MANUALS

Plan is an ambiguous term. It can be as directional as a roadmap and as detailed as a manual. In order to become more responsive and successful, organizations need to move away from plans that act as manuals and focus on building roadmaps and logic models. Rather than dictating specific actions, these approaches give people the tools they need to make quicker and better decisions on their own.

Just think of the technology startup world. Many startups don't even write business plans anymore. Instead they are focused on building prototypes and testing them with customers for real feedback.

There are a variety of models for this type of planning. IDEO's Design Thinking approach, Eric Ries's Lean Startup methodology, Toyota Production System's evolution to lean production, or even some of the more complex organizational models like Frederic Laloux's teal organization—all of these follow a similar theory of action that focuses on learning, doing, and measuring in iterative cycles.

Lean in this context doesn't refer to a lack of frills or management fat. In Ries's (2011) book *The Lean Startup* he describes the build-measure-learn feedback loop methodology, which focuses on launching a "minimum viable product" and learning as quickly as possible.

These ideas can seem antithetical to everything we've learned. Since we were in elementary school, we've been indoctrinated to focus on defining all the parameters of a problem with a single correct solution. These other approaches to planning and problem solving fundamentally accept ambiguity as part of the process—and the execution.

After reading retired General Stanley McChrystal's (2015) book *Team of Teams: New Rules of Engagement for a Complex World*, which describes his command and model for remaking of the Joint Special Operations Task Force in 2004, Anthony had the opportunity to interview Devin Diao, an infantry assault man in the Marine Corps during McChrystal's tenure. Anthony wanted to know how McChrystal's perspective influenced Devin's actual, on-the-ground experience while he was in Afghanistan.

Devin explained that in the military there are standard operating procedures (SOPs), basically step-by-step instructions to perform specific functions. For example, there was an SOP that detailed how to set up a rucksack. In the past, he explained, "If you were going out on a mission, regardless of what you were going to do, you would have a standard pack. If you had a specialized role, you might have a slightly different pack but you didn't have an opportunity to make decisions."

As McChrystal started implementing changes, Devin, as an individual, was able to make adjustments to the SOP for what he packed. He could use the gear list as a guide, not a total given. If he was out on patrol and felt the need to carry more ammunition, he could; he could drop weight by not taking other things.

The rucksack was a small example of a bigger trend during McChrystal's tenure—the ability to make smart adjustments to SOPs allowed Devin and others like him to tailor their approach to their conditions and needs for success.

While education isn't war, futures are on the line and there is a common lesson to be learned. Each district, each school, and each classroom has a unique set of variables that is ever changing. Why expect one plan or one standard operating procedure to work in all contexts?

In our school environments, when plans get so detailed, like a curriculum pacing guide that spells out every action a teacher must take on a specific day, it can be stifling and, depending on your experience, demotivating. New teachers may feel safe with something so prescriptive day to day, but the strategies won't be reaching every student across the spectrum in a meaningful way. Master teachers might see these fixed plans as questioning their experience and may completely ignore the material. By setting a vision and allowing people to have leeway in deciding how to get there, you strengthen results and morale at the same time.

USE CADENCES AND PIVOT POINTS, NOT JUST SCHEDULES AND DEADLINES

In today's rapidly changing world, a plan's value has an immediate half-life—it's dated before it's fully underway. If we focus on planning as a process, not just plans as static products, we prime ourselves to evolve and change. Rather than measuring plans against schedules and deadlines, we can think of plans in terms of cadences and pivot points.

> *If we focus on planning as a process, not just plans as static products, we prime ourselves to evolve and change.*

Deadlines are designed to be fixed, while cadences are intended to evolve. It's true that some dates are not fungible. Deadlines for grants, fundraising benefits, standardized tests, vacations, and the like are structures we must incorporate into planning. Well-defined and explicit deadlines create a sense of security and can help us prioritize actions. However, not all deadlines are grounded in reality. Many are set long in advance during planning phases and are based on nebulous assumptions. Often we end up working on something because we committed to it, not because it is the most important thing we can do for our organizations at that moment.

Instead of an overreliance on deadlines, we can build in a regular cadence to evaluate progress and to pivot if needed. Think about the example of planning a trip. Some of us plan every detail in advance. We book all accommodations, determine activities, and produce a detailed and fixed itinerary. Others take a more plan-and-evolve approach. You might compile a prioritized list of things you want to see and do during your trip. Based on this information you might create a route and select potential places to stay overnight. In order to be flexible, you might decide not to make all your reservations in advance. For places with fixed dates (say, for a concert) or limited hotel options, you might make some reservations ahead of time and defer other decisions for as long as possible to keep options open. Interestingly, both plans require planning time upfront, but the trips differ in the way they are executed and revised along the way.

Back to our schools and district offices, we might plan for short sprints of work with reflection points around each turn. Instead of outlining every measure, we can place emphasis on outlining a guiding vision of success and the early warning signs that might indicate we're off track.

In *The Lean Startup,* Ries (2011) also identified the concept of the pivot, a course correction designed to test a new hypothesis about a plan. If the planning and desired results aren't working or meeting expectations—the festival is booked; it's high season and prices are sky-high—then it's time to pivot. We refer to this ability to pivot as *responsiveness* and see it is a key measure of any successful school or organization.

We have to realize that we can't predict every move in the future. The more open and responsive our planning, the faster we can adapt and pivot. That's why it's wise to avoid putting too much value into Gantt charts or other detailed project plans. These tools are useful to understand the whole picture, but they have to be maintained with learning and iteration in mind. Otherwise, assumptions made in projecting the future will be quickly invalidated.

> We have to realize that we can't predict every move in the future. The more open and responsive our planning, the faster we can adapt and pivot.

ENCOURAGE TESTING, EXPERIMENTS, AND RESPONSIVENESS

Schools want to be innovative but are often afraid to try due to the possibility of failure. We forget that innovation requires experimentation and learning, and learning goes hand in hand with failing. Under the banner of innovation but with the goal of avoiding failure, there can actually be increased control and rigidity.

For example, in an effort to increase autonomy and innovation, one school district decided to put more control for the budget into the hands of principals. The logic behind the move was to empower principals to make budget decisions with their unique schools in mind. But fears of mismanagement along with a desire for more community involvement led the state to require that community boards also approve budget decisions. Although for the most part these boards were well intentioned, legislating oversight stymied the original purpose of increasing autonomy and innovation and led to bottlenecks, politicking, and general confusion.

A better approach might have been to set the budget parameters for principals and allow them to experiment with spending, reporting, and decision making in short cycles that could be reviewed. The principals could try different ways of involving staff and community in spending choices and adapting the approach to fit the needs of the students. The principals could learn and iterate, and the community wouldn't fear that spending would get out of hand.

In the context of classrooms, teachers can be encouraged to experiment with how to adapt techniques, materials, and technology to different situations and students and how to make changes based on insights they get from observations and data.

Demanding that teachers implement a reading program with fidelity may mean they comply fully with the letter of the program, but it doesn't ensure the quality of student learning. The best-case result is that you get uniformity in classrooms; the worse and more likely scenario is that natural differences in the way students learn aren't accommodated by the reading program and all students suffer.

Often when you are on the frontlines, whether you are a soldier on the battlefield or a teacher in a school, confronting specifications or requirements that are generic and not specific enough to the situation makes it illogical to comply. In the case of a soldier, it could lead to life or death.

Schools and organizations will continue to struggle to perfect the right level of tight and loose in these situations, but *planning for change, not perfection* helps create the space for experimenting, learning, and responsiveness to the actual needs of students and the larger purpose.

EXPERIMENTS

Experimenting With Planning

Remember: Experiments are designed as trials to be tested out, iterated, studied, and broadly implemented over time. Try out and adapt the experiments on planning to fit your role and context.

What follows are some simple, practical steps to guide you as you begin to follow the New Rule: *Plan for change, not perfection.* You can think of them as changes from the "ground up" that you can affect in your own role, planning, and teams without waiting for larger-scale efforts. If you begin to shift your own assumptions, language, and practices around planning, you'll experience real shifts in the way you—and the people around you—work.

EXPERIMENT 1
Define a Clear Purpose

A simple definition of purpose is "the ideal state we wish to achieve." We typically reserve purpose statements for large initiatives and organizational initiatives, but defining a purpose is useful for all the work we do. When embarking on any project—on our own, with a team, or even at the whole-organization level—start with a quick mental exercise and ask, "What is the purpose of this work?"

Using the tips provided, in just a few minutes you can come up with a usable purpose that will provide guidance and clarity when you have to make decisions.

1. **Paint a picture of success.** If the purpose is to be a North Star, it must provide a guiding vision. Brainstorm and discuss ideas by asking yourself questions like these:

    What would success look like?

    What's the ideal state I am trying to achieve?

    When I am done with this work, what do I hope will be true?

    For example, let's say you are a school principal and you have heard that several of your top teachers are planning to leave next year. You know this will leave a hole in your instructional team. You want to take on a project to recruit and retain great talent at your school. You ask yourself the questions on the previous page and determine an ideal state might be the following:

> *Highly motivated teachers feel personally and professionally aligned with the school and decide to stay and work here.*

This is a great starting purpose. It's easy to imagine, and it's inspiring and ambitious. When you close your eyes you can see and feel what this looks like, including identifying highly motivated teachers, brainstorming ways for teachers to feel personally connected with the school, discovering how to align the school with the professional goals of strong teachers, and asking great teachers to stay and work here. A great purpose paints such a clear picture that it's easy to think of ways to start working toward that vision.

Painting a picture of success is also a great vehicle to communicate purpose. By sharing the statement above, you can solicit targeted feedback and reactions. This might be the most important step. Can people see this picture of success coming true? Does it provide a clear North Star to work toward? Now is the time to get clear and aligned.

2. **Get specific about impact.** As you can see from the purpose example above, a purpose statement begins with a clear vision of success. For many planning activities this could be enough. If you are looking to supercharge your purpose, adding in the impact can help with inspiration and gives the purpose more context. Ask, "What impact will this have on our team and organization?"

School project: Teacher recruitment and retention

Purpose: Highly motivated teachers feel personally and professionally aligned with the school and decide to stay and work here.

Impact: Students have the opportunity to build meaningful long-term relationships and grow with and alongside teachers.

---

3. **Avoid action items.** Notice that the purpose does not prescribe specific actions or a to-do list. It doesn't say, "Creating a program

that doubles retention" or "Rolling out an initiative that incentivizes employee referrals." Part of creating a purpose is setting a vision of success without defining how the team will get there. This frees up the team to be creative in their approach and responsive to the needs they uncover.

4. **Apply the Goldilocks principle.** In the famous fairy tale, the girl finds the bear's porridge that isn't too hot, isn't too cold, but is just right. You want to avoid a purpose statement that is too generic or too prescriptive. For example:

Too broad: Parent engagement

Too specific: Parents are engaged through monthly newsletters, weekly emails, and quarterly in-person events.

Just right: Parents are engaged in multiple ways that allow them to access information as easily as possible.

5. **Use it—make purpose part of your plan.** After you create a purpose, it's important to use it. When executing a plan ask, "Is this direction (or decision) in line with our team's purpose?" When someone comes to you asking for feedback or advice, use this simple question to refocus a discussion around the most important guidepost—the team or project purpose. By referencing and using the purpose often, you bring the purpose statement to life, rather than it being a relic or artifact of early team creation.

EXPERIMENT 2

Delineate Between What You Know and What You Anticipate

During the planning process people can get caught up arguing over things they don't even know for sure are true. Instead of relying on assumptions, guide your plans with data from real experiences. When you embrace the motto "start by starting," you can skip the anticipation game and refine your plan as you learn and iterate. In other words, move forward with what you know, and decide later what to adjust and how.

Let's extend the example of a teacher retention program. Here are some of the possible actions in the plan:

- Identify highly motivated teachers.

- Brainstorm ways for teachers to feel personally connected to the school.

- Discover how to align the school with the professional goals of strong teachers.

- Ask great teachers to stay and work here.

While planning out the steps, you might get worried about the distinction between "highly motivated" teachers and the rest. You may be concerned that by singling out a group of teachers, others could feel left behind. For that you can ask yourself:

Do I know this is going to happen, or am I anticipating harm will happen?

What do you know? (based on presently known information and experiences)	What are you anticipating? (based on what might happen or could happen)
Several teachers have mentioned that explicitly asking them to stay would increase the likelihood that they will consider staying.	Teachers who aren't asked to stay will develop malicious feelings toward the school, and their performance will suffer as a result.

The issue in the right-hand column might feel worrisome, but you don't know it will happen. Rather than trying to plan around these decisions, or argue over their validity, you can delay addressing them until you have further information. Just make sure you revisit the plan as often as needed to pivot once you do gather experiences and data.

For example, after the first communications, you might get feedback that people are confused about why certain teachers are getting individual invitations to stay on. This may lead you to reassess and shift directions. People can rest assured that this plan is more realistic because it doesn't rely on artificial assumptions (which we know will all be ignored or changed).

Once you begin using this simple skill, you will see ways to apply it everywhere.

. . . .

Planning Is Working When . . .

As with any successful planning, we want to leave you with a vision of success. At the most basic level, a simple measure of successful planning is how often a plan gets referenced. When a plan is meaningful, it is used as touchstone and guide. People at all levels refer to it frequently as they talk about and navigate their next steps and the decisions they are making. It guides everyone's communication, contributing to a sense that people are on the same page. We know planning is working when . . .

There's a greater sense of being alive. When planning sets the direction but is open enough to encourage change and evolution, the process feels aspirational but real enough to inspire action. Responsive planning doesn't feel like an exercise in futility.

Teams and organizations have a clear and motivating purpose. Many organizations talk about purpose, but it's much rarer for purpose to be an organizing framework. In a plan-and-evolve environment, planning clarifies purpose up front and empowers people to be guided by a larger vision, instead of sticking to a predetermined plan-and-control set of actions or timelines. A clear and motivating purpose inspires learning and iteration, and it lessens the fear of being judged, wrong, or less capable.

Everyone is continuously evolving, improving, and aiming higher. When planning is open, iterative, and relieved of the need for perfection, each person is empowered to take actions that are responsive to current reality. You can see students and teachers approach learning with more openness and enthusiasm. The ultimate result is that students and teachers make more progress toward goals and learn much more along the way.

. . . .

CHAPTER 2

Teaming

Build Trust and Allow Authority to Spread

How does it feel when you walk through a workplace that is mostly closed-door offices and high-walled cubicles versus a workplace that is open, with shared space?

Organizations are moving toward more open physical spaces for a reason. Information, knowledge, and solutions are no longer on the shoulders of individuals and bosses but on teams.

As organizations implement practices that require more responsiveness, quicker alignment, and faster decision making, teams—not autocratic bosses—are becoming the units of change in organizations. They are the groups that are formed—and disbanded—to respond to conditions, solve problems, and achieve the larger purpose everyone is aiming for.

But what are teams and how can we get the best from them? Are they merely a bunch of colleagues coming together to work collaboratively? Or are there particular characteristics that lead to the benefits we hope for in terms of engagement, speed, expertise, creativity, and results? Does a focus on teaming transform the employee experience from a traditional hierarchical organization, or is it just more meetings?

> Teams—not autocratic bosses—are becoming the units of change in organizations.

For our purposes, effective teaming is only in small part about organizational structure. More significantly, it's about team dynamics themselves. To illustrate, we can look at two opposite types of cultures and organizations—the military and the movie business.

General Stanley McChrystal (2015) shares in his book *Team of Teams* that when he took command of the Joint Special Operations Task Force in 2004, he and his team quickly realized that conventional military tactics were failing in the fight against Al Qaeda in Iraq:

> Just as the cohort of young people born in the 1990s and 2000s are considered "digital natives" in contrast to their "digital immigrants" parents, AQI (Al Qaeda in Iraq) was an organization native to the information-rich, densely interconnected world of the twenty-first century. It operated in ways that diverged radically from those we thought of as "correct" and "effective." (pp. 19–20)

McChrystal explains that the task force had to rebuild the way it was structured and how it worked by "swapping our sturdy architecture for organic fluidity, because it was the only way to confront a rising tide of complex threats" (p. 20). The restructuring was based on the concepts of extremely transparent information sharing, called *shared consciousness*, and decentralized decision-making authority, called *empowered execution*.

On the opposite end of the organizational spectrum is Hollywood. We associate filmmaking with powerful film studios who bring legions of talented individuals together to fulfill their vision. But the industry has changed dramatically, from one where all the power and control was housed within the movie studios to one where the power is being distributed to producers who put together teams for each project. This process is known as the Hollywood model of project management (Davidson, 2015).

In the Hollywood model, a team is assembled to lead all of the moving parts. They work together until the project is completed, and then the team is disbanded. The team members are recruited based on their experience, availability, and particular skills, and each person has very specific roles and accountabilities.

> *"[We rebuilt the way we were structured and how we worked by] swapping our sturdy architecture for organic fluidity, because it was the only way to confront a rising tide of complex threats."*
>
> *—General Stanley McChrystal*

Each team is figuring how to get their piece of the work done, including what processes they are going to use, the amount of information or feedback they need from other teams or the director, and the decisions they need to make in order to fulfill the specific, agreed-upon purpose of the team. For instance, if you're the casting agent, other people and teams are relying on you and your team to get your part of the job done to achieve the vision. That might mean determining the way auditions are handled; figuring out the budget for "talent," including stars and newcomers; and getting insight and feedback from the director or producers. The casting agent doesn't seek consensus from the set designers and the location managers.

Organizations are constantly trying to improve productivity and the effectiveness of their teams. General McChrystal put new and more effective standard operating procedures (SOPs) in place within the military. Hollywood thrives on autonomous hubs made up of uniquely skilled individuals who are assembled for each project.

These diverse organizations are thriving. So if we want our schools to be more alive, responsive, and effective, what's getting in our way?

 ## The Problem

While teams are the future, they aren't a magic bullet. Teams suffer from several dysfunctions that limit their effectiveness.

- First, teams tend to be formed based on a shared point of view. When teams are focused on areas of collective knowledge and agreement, they are apt to overlook the unique knowledge held by individual team members, even when the individual information may offer more valuable or needed insight. This consensus orientation can result in groupthink.

- Second, authority on teams is still held at the top. It's no longer about designated hierarchies and access to people and information. In fact, access has been flattened. The ease of access—whether in reference to students, colleagues, parents, or communities—puts everyone on the frontlines, literally and figuratively. Even so, opinions by high-status people tend to override knowledge from on-the-ground roles, even when those roles have access to better data and information.

- Third, teams are hard to change. Once a team has been formed, it takes on a life of its own. In a world where change is speeding up, teams need to be more structurally fluid and easy to disband.

Working in teams is the new norm, but our understanding of how to maximize their effectiveness is still largely shaped by the legacy of hierarchical organizations with an emphasis on top-down control rather than team-based autonomy and evolution. We need new ground rules for how authority operates in teams and how to reap the benefits of this responsive structure.

> *We need new ground rules for how authority operates in teams and how to reap the benefits of this responsive structure.*

WE'RE DRAGGED DOWN BY THE SLOW AND UNWIELDY LEGACY OF HIERARCHIES

Highly functioning, well-designed teams bring the best of different skills into one cohesive unit. Unfortunately, teams in the current structures are often constrained by the hierarchies they live within. In the 20th century, when information was less abundant and iterations were slower, the hierarchy of the typical organizational chart made sense with command-and-control decisions distributed from the top.

Some people would argue that the current organizational chart is a manifestation of the classic feudal system where there was always competition and intrigue among neighboring kings for power and terrain.

This was the de facto model throughout the Analog Age, which basically carried us through the Industrial Age into the start of the Digital Age in the 1970s, which began with the introduction of the personal computer. It's the period when information traveled in sequential patterns rather than in flexible networks.

Think about it in terms of an audiocassette, a VHS tape, an analog (dial face) watch, or a textbook. In an analog world, a fixed sequence of information is presented regardless of the interests or needs of the individual reader or observer. In a digital environment, this is all changed. A world of networked connections, including the cloud, enables us to access content in dynamic, nonlinear categories. For example, with Netflix not only can you select from an

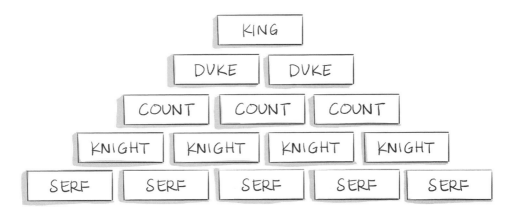

unlimited number of movies but you can quickly jump to specific scenes in a movie or recommendations of related movies. Your digital photos can be stored in multiple organizational relationships, including time/date, location, event, people tagged, and so on. This networked world is quickly dominating our expectations for how things should work.

So, going back to our schools and districts, what does this mean? The cascade of a typical organization chart, with its sequential and hierarchical reporting lines, fixed departmental alliances,

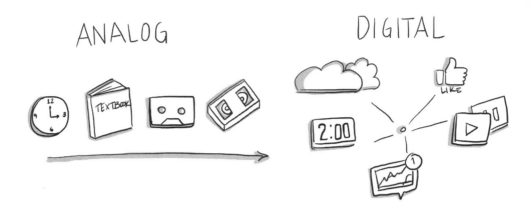

and lack of information flow between silos, follows the slow and unwieldy Analog Age—and no longer fits our networked Digital Age lives. This legacy organizational approach reduces efficiency, and its rigidity can affect overall morale. In fact, Jack Welch, the legendary CEO of GE, began advocating for "boundaryless organizations" twenty-five years ago. Perhaps he was ahead of his time, but it's now urgent that we find new models of responsiveness to match our networked Digital Age.

> *The cascade of a typical organization chart . . . follows the slow and unwieldy Analog Age—and no longer fits our networked Digital Age lives.*

To improve collaboration, "matrixed" organization structures have been tried. Those are the traditional hierarchies with "dotted line" reporting between departments designed to bridge silos. In our school districts, this can look like departments that interact with a lot of other departments, such as the Title 1 office, the office of accountability, and the instructional coaching teams. Unfortunately, research by Ethan Bernstein, professor of organizational behavior at Harvard, has shown the result is usually more complexity and more meetings, rather than more responsiveness and more effective problem solving and decision making (Bernstein & Nohria, 1991/2016).

This isn't an abstract issue for organizational experts and consultants. The hierarchal underpinnings of our school cultures means we miss out on the power of digital networks. Rather than accessing the information, expertise, and insight of the best person or team, we focus on gatekeepers, chains of authority, and friends who can help us get something done, because often we aren't even aware of who's doing what and whether possible solutions or services already exist.

Imagine you're a parent with a student getting intervention services. How can you have comprehensive conversations about your child's experience when there are so many different departments? Your primary contact might be the Intervention office under the direction of Student Support, but Customer Service is under Family Relationships and you might need or benefit from some of the programs they offer without ever knowing about them. Or there might be technology that could help—or that's not working—and input from Ed Tech might have solutions for your child, again, without you knowing that such a department even exists.

And you can't rely on the school contacts to know about all these options either. They may be on a team or have a matrixed relationship with some of the related departments, which gives them knowledge of some additional services. However, to figure out others, they would need to ask their boss, who would call another boss, who would raise the issue at an upcoming meeting—if they remembered. Many schools worry about the chaos that would ensue if individual teachers and staff were to start reaching out directly in a networked fashion to build connections and solutions—and then share them more widely.

In a world where "customers" expect to get answers and solutions—and have the ability to complain in public, independently access data, and organize and connect online—a siloed organization will only create frustration and distrust. For the family accessing specialized learning services, this linear approach doesn't seem authoritative and professional; it seems unresponsive, slow, and impersonal. We need to move toward creating VIP learning experiences for every child and family—and for the teachers and staff who want to do their best work.

LAND GRABS ARE STILL TOO COMMON

We've been trained to believe that having more responsibility and more people reporting to us leads to job security and relevance. In a siloed organization, we need more responsibility and more people to manage in order to get the resources and information we need to get things done without relying on others. Each of these silos develops its own cultures and operating processes, which can easily go against the grain of the organization and its larger purpose, encouraging people to build yet larger fiefdoms to operate within.

Take a look at the organizational chart of a large school district. They have a customer service department and communications department under Family Relations. Imagine the quality of service you would receive if you called the customer service department about a school your child is attending. Doesn't each school provide its own customer service?

The highly siloed structure we see in school districts is often the regional or area superintendents' hierarchy. In many cases, area superintendents, not principals, have direct command over their schools and may have budgets larger than the district office. You can imagine that you would want to build out your reach to get your work done, rather than relying on shared services and departments and coordination with other silos with different cultures and ways of doing things.

It's possible you've been part of a reorganization or a growing organization where you've had the opportunity to help design the organizational chart. In that case, you have firsthand knowledge of how organizational charts—like strategic plans—are static snapshots of roles and accountabilities that become obsolete as soon as they are created. With work evolving so quickly, the need for flexibility in addressing problems increases, but the entrenched reporting structures can get in the way. If the organization chart says one thing, there isn't a mechanism—or the trust—to work outside these fiefdoms. Without the trust that comes with more interaction and responsiveness across boundaries, the land-grab mentality can take over.

Analog Age Organizational Chart of a Large Urban School District

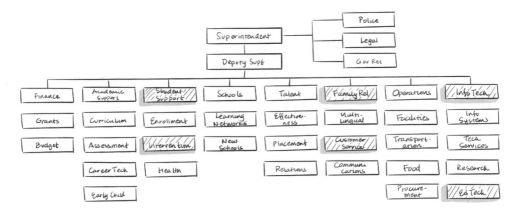

THE NEW SCHOOL RULES

What we find is that while having more turf and more people in our domain might satisfy our egos—that is, if we're the bosses—it doesn't lead to better results. Departments and teams become isolated, lack perspective, and can start serving the fiefdom rather than the larger purpose. Advocating for resources and maintaining and expanding turf can take precedence over fulfilling the vision and collaborating with the best people available—regardless of their position on the organization chart.

> *Without the trust that comes with more interaction and responsiveness across boundaries, the land-grab mentality can take over.*

WHEN EVERYONE AND NO ONE IS RESPONSIBLE

Our understanding of how to operate in teams is still largely shaped in response to the legacy of hierarchical organizations and a focus on top-down power. As our organizational units transition into teams, we don't have a map for how to operate these smaller units of authority. In the confusion, many teams will default to team consensus as a model to move work forward.

On the surface, team consensus can be appealing. You might think, "I want everyone on my team to have a say in the decision" or "I want us to work together and use consensus." There's nothing wrong with these sentiments, and it's true that work benefits from multiple perspectives. Where this approach goes wrong is when we equate a sense of engagement and commitment with equal roles and equal say. Lessons from group psychology and management theory clearly show that "when everyone is responsible, no one is responsible" and work suffers as a result.

Responsive teams are made up of individuals with roles and specific accountabilities that fit the needs of the team and its purpose. Even though all team members might have valuable perspective, there needs to be clear decision-making authority to move work forward.

> *Even though all team members might have valuable perspective, there needs to be clear decision-making authority to move work forward.*

If we equate collaboration, equality, and "being nice" with positive team culture, we might avoid seeking clear accountability and authority to make decisions. Or everyone defers to everyone else and no one has a sense of urgency to move the work forward or really owns the various decisions that need to be made. Tension, confusion, and hurt feelings can take on an even larger role in spite of everyone's good intentions.

⬡ NEW RULE — The New Rule

Build Trust and Allow Authority to Spread

The most effective teams give us a sense of belonging, engagement, and making a difference. Teams that don't work promise collaboration and nimbleness but end up feeling like sideshows to the "real" meetings with the higher-ups who really make the decisions.

In responsive organizations, effective teams are powerful units of change. They depend on trust and meaningful authority in an environment where they can act almost as small startups within the larger organization. These high-functioning and responsive teams exist in a network with other teams, giving them access to the information they need to make decisions. They are structurally fluid, expanding and contracting with new information.

> In responsive organizations, effective teams are powerful units of change. . . . They can act almost as small startups within the larger organization.

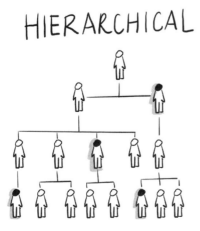

HIERARCHICAL

NODE

One of the important features of responsive teams is that they are structured like nodes in a network instead of stations in a rigid sequence. One of the characteristics of network nodes is that they have their own purpose, individual accountabilities, autonomy, and authority. In other words, the bosses and leaders no longer command the pieces on the board. Instead, guided by the purpose of the team, project, and larger initiative, these nodes operate relatively independently but are connected to other teams to inform and support each other, while constantly seeking new connections needed to achieve the team's purpose.

For many, this model of teams and teaming can be a jolt to the system. Letting go of the control and allowing teams to drive their own path can feel like you're taking off the training wheels on your child's bike for the first time. When your child falls, it's your job to give her the confidence to get back up. When she succeeds in getting from point A to point B, you will continue to set up new goals like riding farther, faster, or down a small hill.

> *Letting go of the control and allowing teams to drive their own path can feel like you're taking off the training wheels on your child's bike for the first time.*

In the workplace, dealing with the anxiety of "taking off the training wheels" is a process that follows the New Rule: *Build trust and allow authority to spread*. It means letting go of control and letting others take the lead in order to learn by doing and experimenting, even when their decisions differ from the decisions you would make.

Letting go of, or distributing, authority is fundamentally different than what we traditionally think of as delegation. With delegation, responsibility is *entrusted* to another team or person, typically one less senior, in order to fulfill a task. However, the ultimate *authority* to make decisions lies with the delegator. If the more junior person makes a decision that doesn't align with the more senior person's preferences, the delegator can easily step in and override the decision or threaten to take back authority. In the hierarchical model, good leaders aim to grant some degree of authority to

> *In the hierarchical model, good leaders aim to grant some degree of authority to their staff and teams, but this authority is typically contingent—it's a grant and can be taken back at any moment. This dynamic erodes trust and doesn't allow authority to spread.*

their staff and teams, but again, this authority is typically contingent—it's a grant and can be taken back at any moment. This dynamic erodes trust and doesn't allow authority to spread.

Instead of granting contingent authority through delegation, the model of distributing authority to teams in a meaningful way frees them up to make decisions quickly in response to emerging data and information.

In *The NEW School Rules* the concept of distributed authority is distinct from the practice of distributed leadership, which is often referenced in educational leadership books. In *Distributed Leadership*, Spillane (2006) defines leadership as any "activities tied to the core work of the organization that are designed by organizational members to influence the motivation, knowledge, affect, or practices of other organizational members" (pp. 11–12). In *The NEW School Rules*, instead of focusing on influencing others to do work, we focus on distributing the authority to make decisions and drive work within teams.

A model of distributed authority looks like this:

- Teams have a clear, shared purpose that aligns with the organization's vision and planning.

- Members of the team have authority to make decisions that serve the purpose of their team and organization.

- Each person's responsibilities are transparent and specific to the needs of that team and are not based on the hierarchy of the organization chart.

- Teams act like nodes, with meaningful, trusted connections across the organization, allowing them to access and redistribute information as needed to move work forward.

- Teams evolve to fulfill their purpose, including changing members, refining the purpose, disbanding as needs evolve, or spanning new nodes for new work to be done.

The clarity of purpose, roles, and authority allow the organization to trust that the work will get done without needing layers of oversight and approval. Let's take a look at these strategies at play in the case study of a southeastern city school district.

· ·

CASE STUDY

Case Study: Building an Organization Around Team Purpose, Not Existing Hierarchies

The inspiration to create a more responsive and nimble way of working often starts when a big change is on the horizon. That could be a major grant, a lagging report card, or a new strategic plan. The superintendent can continue as before—approaching the latest reform effort with the old command-and-control approach. Or it can become a moment to change *how* the work is done as well as the specifics of the educational plans.

This particular major city school district received a federal grant in 2012 to implement competency-based instructional models and a culture where students own their learning. The district had gotten off to a good start. A new team had been created, detailed planning and documentations were underway, and vendors to support the work were being evaluated. However, there were two looming problems:

1. It seemed that school leaders and teachers had no idea how to integrate this new instructional initiative into the dozen or so other initiatives that were already underway. In fact, there was substantial pushback, and it appeared that individual schools were ignoring efforts to begin the implementation.

2. Due to continued conflict around equity and politics, there were signs of significant organizational unrest within the district. Turnover of senior leaders was on the rise. In 2014, the superintendent of seven years resigned and an eight-month search for a new superintendent began. In 2015, the board selected Gloria, a veteran superintendent with a tremendous track record at another county school district. She had been named superintendent of the year and was a member of the governing board of the American Association of School Administrators.

Gloria walked into a district where there were a lot of silos, limited transparency, and very little alignment of focus. It was unclear who was doing what in the district office, and the student achievement gap had continued to grow. One of the key changes Gloria made to the existing cabinet was to get rid of it. Instead of an exclusive cabinet, a new inclusive team, called the Integration Team, was put together with people of all levels. There were district office leaders, school principals, and several school team–level participants representing different functional areas of the district. Everyone had a voice based on their role and experience. The purpose of the team was to share ideas, learn as a group, build trust, and define the work to be done.

One of the first things the Integration Team took on was getting everyone aligned on the district's strategic plan and purpose: "to provide challenging education choices to increase achievement and close achievement gaps, to prepare all students to compete in a global economy and make positive contributions to our community and nation." They began by making sure everyone on the Integration Team was clear and on the same page and then spreading that message and focus into the schools and their community. Early on, to reset the way they all interacted, they looked for ways to humanize their meetings, allowing for funny things to happen to make people authentic and vulnerable instead of adhering to pomp and circumstance.

Simultaneously, they began to use their Integration Team meetings to model what they expected from teaching and learning in the schools and classrooms. In the past, decisions were won or lost by people with the loudest voice and the most power. Now decisions would be tested against the top organizational goals, and options around each decision would be discussed in groups based on like and unlike interests.

They adopted a meeting structure that was more dynamic than "updates" and "report outs" on areas of concern. It included successes, positive failures, and lessons learned to expand their thinking and shift their mindsets. Too much focus on the negative and problematic is discouraging and interprets mistakes and failures as bad. Too much focus on the positive is a recipe for following predefined plans and not listening to new information and making adjustments.

This operational change on the Integration Team rippled to other teams, including the federal group. This team was originally created to research and design the district's application for funding. The team created documentation for executing the plans, but with so few people involved in its development, it seemed to be turning into a more and more rigid command-and-control process, with the original design team now in a new role of execution. Instead of building engagement and shared purpose with other teams, it appeared that the approach had resulted in inconsistent and disengaged implementation.

Gloria recognized that new roles with new authority would be needed to carry the work forward to implementation. The lead of the design team became a member of the implementation team as a resource for background and technical information and, eventually, shifted out of the team completely.

New teams were formed to address issues that arose from the ground up instead of assumptions made from the top down. There was so much to be done, but the Integration Team felt that focusing on tangible needs in small increments would give lots of people a foothold and a way to get involved. It would allow trust to spread more quickly.

Evolving the organizational chart, the school district made changes to focus on the work to be done based on the needs from the front lines, instead of allowing the district leaders to build out their fiefdoms. Across the district, teams that had been framed around an individual's agenda versus the organization's goals were disbanded. The personalized learning team grew from a special project or grant team to a district-level team, which closely aligned to the mission of the district. Additional teams were created as separate nodes to focus on implementation and educational equity.

Teams were created with people who were excited about the need or project, who had relevant expertise, and who represented different levels of seniority and hierarchical power in order to expand information sharing and to create small experiments that would allow authority to spread.

Change didn't happen overnight as overwriting old memories and rebuilding trust takes consistent reinforcement. A year into this process, there were signs that the culture of this district had transformed greatly. School leaders and teachers at historically struggling schools appeared to feel capable and empowered. At one particularly meaningful moment, the teachers gave an emotional testimony that they no longer felt like they were constantly being looked down on by the district and like they were victims to changing priorities. With greater cohesion and purpose, turnover slowed, giving everyone confidence that the district office wasn't focused on its own interests but was wholeheartedly in the business of supporting the priorities of the schools, teachers, and most of all the children.

Lessons

Teams within your organization are the nodes that get the work done. They are the small, core communities where organizations let the New Rule take hold: *Build trust and allow authority to spread.*

The way you think about structuring and networking your teams within the organization will determine how well your organization lives its purpose. Here are several cornerstone lessons for the model of teaming where authority is distributed and ideas, experiments, and effective execution come alive:

- Clarify the purpose of every team . . . and revisit it.
- Build trust and address tensions.
- Develop effective team habits that support distributed authority.
- Embrace dynamic team structures that evolve and end.

CLARIFY THE PURPOSE OF EVERY TEAM . . . AND REVISIT IT

Too often we get pulled into project teams where the purpose is assumed and unspoken. For example, you may be invited to a working group called Safety Task Force. The purpose isn't explicitly stated, but it's assumed that this group convenes to talk about safety issues. Weeks or months go by with meeting after meeting. Over time, little shifts go unnoticed, the team grows, and the work changes. One day you show up for yet another meeting and wonder why you are there, or it dawns on you that everyone is working toward different goals. Making assumptions about the purpose of a team, and not publishing or revisiting it, means that the goal fades into obscurity and the team wastes time and resources. Finding the right purpose, making it transparent, and reviewing it regularly can help teams move in the right direction and help individuals decide how they will contribute to the overall goal.

There's an assumption that the purpose of a team, once stated, should be immutable. Teams suffer because of this—frequently limiting the work to fit a limited plan, even when the actual need is clarified or the work shifts and a new direction is needed. Or the team is limited in fulfilling its purpose because the people on the team are no longer the best fit for the work at hand.

In the case study we saw two examples of where Gloria made a deliberate choice to look beyond the formal hierarchy and find the right people for the team purpose. First, she got rid of the legacy cabinet and formed the Integration Team, which included contributors from all levels that could bring to bear diverse perspectives and contributions to the work. Second, in forming the personalized learning team, rather than letting the original designer move into the role of implementation lead, she recognized a different skillset would be needed. The original designer simply played an advisory role and eventually shifted off the team altogether when it no longer served the work.

For a new team, questioning its purpose can easily be skipped over. Imagine the situation of a new team coming together to "evaluate a new learning management system (LMS)." The assumption is probably to pick the best LMS out there. The team gathers requirements, reviews vendors, makes a recommendation, and the system is purchased. Along the way there are questions about implementation and utilization, but it's assumed that the next team will address those issues. At the end of the project, a great product is brought into the schools, but after training and some time for adoption, only 10 percent of the features are actually utilized.

If the team were to look back, perhaps there was a missed opportunity to revisit the purpose. As questions surfaced about implementation, it might have prompted the team to ask, "Is evaluating learning systems what is needed from us right now?"

In this case, they might have discovered the team's purpose should have been focused on defining the problem they were trying to solve with a new LMS. Perhaps the solution was coming before the problem was understood. Did teachers need a multifaceted solution for multiple needs, or did they need a tool to share documents or create curriculum? When a team is focused on the wrong purpose—whether it was assigned to the team or defined by the team—lots of time and money is spent on results that do not matter.

> When a team is focused on the wrong purpose—whether it was assigned to the team or defined by the team—lots of time and money is spent on results that do not matter.

Once the right purpose is defined, it acts as a guidepost, letting team members make autonomous decisions in real time with confidence, knowing they are acting in line with the purpose of the work.

BUILD TRUST AND ADDRESS TENSIONS

After purpose, trust is a cornerstone of effective teams. It's one of those values that gets thrown around but in actuality is very difficult to cultivate. The Google blog and project called re:Work, which is devoted to research and practices for successful teams and making work better, calls it "psychological safety" and "dependability" (Rozovsky, 2015).

Whatever you call it, trust is the glue that holds teams together and separates effective teams from dysfunctional and unsuccessful ones. Trust means you can rely on your colleagues; you can share information honestly without a fear of retribution or personal attack. It means hard things can be brought out in the open— whether it's your own confusion about a direction or decision, conflicts about the process of working together, or disagreement about the purpose or best next steps.

> Trust is the glue that holds teams together and separates effective teams from dysfunctional and unsuccessful ones.

In the book *Holacracy,* author Brian J. Robertson (2015) refers to these types of conflicts and stress as "tensions," which he defines as "the perception of a specific gap between current reality and a sensed potential" (p. 17). A simpler version might be "the feeling that there is a gap between the way things are and the way things could be."

Rather than thinking about tension negatively, Robertson repurposes tension and describes it as a natural

> Tension: The feeling that there is a gap between the way things are and the way things could be.

by-product of a growing and evolving organization. Whether you call it tension, friction, or strain, the fact remains that it's inevitable. In fact, only organizations that are stagnating don't have tensions—no one is caring enough or pushing enough to create stress.

That said, even when we think about it this way, it's still easier to ignore these feelings than to surface them. But you can't rely on someone else to bring up issues on your behalf, and if you ignore tension you may be missing an opportunity to evolve the organization in a positive direction.

Saying "I feel a tension about this" recognizes that you're sensing a gap that may not be universal but is important to address for your needs and role.

Conversely, saying "There's a problem" or "I have a problem" not only has a more negative connotation but also can be perceived as a universal statement of fact, when others may not sense the same problem at all. From a strategic communications standpoint, if you are trying to work with others, focusing on your personal experience rather than finger-pointing indicated by a "problem" can be helpful for keeping defenses low and keeping people open to hearing what comes next. You might use other language in your organization. We've had teams use *stress, discomfort,* or related terms. The important thing is to make sure it's safe to raise issues and to have shared, nonblaming language that everyone understands.

Trust exists on two levels in responsive organizations. First, as we describe above, is the trust between individuals on teams. The purpose and goals of the team come first, and team members commit to productively surfacing tension instead of avoiding it or sweeping it under the rug. Having

> Only organizations that are stagnating don't have tensions—no one is caring enough or pushing enough to create stress.

trust within a team means important discussions happen directly with the group, not in side meetings, campaigning, and gossip.

The second level—within an organization and especially between teams—is equally important. It means that information flows between groups and is accessible as needed. Communication takes place about what teams are doing and what help or input they might need. This type of organizational trust acknowledges that other teams are doing work that is as good and important as your team's, and they are doing it with the best information they have to get the work done.

One type of trust without the other will not serve the organization. Someone who trusts only their team and is suspicious of other teams will hoard information or land-grab, standing in the way of achieving the collective purpose. Same for the inverse. Someone who believes in the greater mission and teams of an organization but distrusts their own team will not be able to move their work forward. Cultivating trust on both levels is particularly important when you work in an organization that is continuously evolving and ending teams as needed.

Think of ways to foster connections, share experiences, and know each other as colleagues and individuals. (You never know what passions, skills, and experiences someone has that might contribute to a project or could enrich your relationship.) In the case study the Integration Team found ways to inject humor and authenticity into meetings. Most importantly, make sure teams are focused on the right things and have the autonomy to achieve wins together. Gloria focused on achieving tangible wins in small increments to give people a foothold and a way to get involved. There is no more important trust-building activity than achieving success together.

DEVELOP EFFECTIVE TEAM HABITS THAT SUPPORT DISTRIBUTED AUTHORITY

Purpose and trust give teams meaningful direction based on shared goals rather than strong personalities and hierarchies. But equally important are a team's regular habits. Responsive teams don't rely on some outside command-and-control authority figure to define and structure the work. That means team members must take ownership and drive their own work. It's exciting but also demanding.

There are several habits to pay attention to:

1. **Team transparency.** Transparency builds trust, clarity, and confidence. If you have different ideas of about who is doing what and why, or you don't know, your

> Team members must take ownership and drive their own work.

team can't work as an effective unit. You can't communicate well with other teams. You can't support each other.

Each team needs to find its best practices for maintaining transparency. That can be weekly check-ins, e-mail or platform-based updates, metric reports, and more periodic, open-ended discussions.

A great example of team transparency is sharing meaningful metrics. If you are working on a team where the purpose is to "understand the need for a districtwide learning management system," one meaningful metric might be "percentage of teachers who responded to a survey." Let's say you have a weekly team check-in meeting where you hold the first 10 minutes for reporting on metrics. The person in charge of gathering survey responses reports that only 10 percent of teachers have responded to the survey.

This triggers important questions from the rest of the team: "How can we make decisions with limited data?" and "How can we help increase the response rate so we feel confident moving forward?" This level of transparency gives access to all team members and helps resolve sticky issues so people can move forward with their work confidently.

2. **Meeting protocols and facilitators.** One of the benefits of the traditional top-down structure is that there is one person who is the authority figure. In an autonomous team environment, one of the downsides is that it is easy for meetings to become long, unruly forums for every person to weigh in.

A protocol—a shared SOP, or standard operating procedure—for team communication and meetings can provide that structure, just like following the rules of a board game. What's important with meeting protocols is that everyone needs to agree on the protocol. (See Experiment 4 at the end of the chapter for some specific recommendations you can begin with.)

Additionally, meetings have a facilitator to make sure people follow the protocol. The facilitator plays a supporting role to help prevent side issues and debates from taking people down a rabbit hole and making sure all voices are heard.

Meeting protocols can be used for the following:

- kick-off meetings for initial team planning

- check-in meetings to support team transparency

- process meetings to build in review of issues regarding the team itself, including the makeup of the team and team members, team building, team structure and interactions with other teams, unresolved decisions or conflicts, and so on

- brainstorming and retreat meetings to do bigger-picture thinking

3. **Doing the work.** Meetings are great to align teams and remove barriers, but the most important habit is actually getting the work done outside of meetings.

You can gauge how well you and your team are "doing the work" by asking, "How empowered does your team feel about getting work done and making decisions autonomously or in small work sessions?"

This might sound like a simple question, but a team can easily be sidelined by an overly restrictive culture where team members feel the need to run every decision up to the team leader, maintaining the familiar hierarchy. Even more innocuous is the dynamic that occurs when people are expected to do an aspect of the work, but their authority is unclear. This leaves people feeling like they need to default to total consensus and consulting everyone before making a decision.

If work isn't getting done, if meetings are the default and nothing significant is happening in between, it's a good sign that roles, authority, and the purpose are unclear—or the tasks and expectations are too big or vague. (We'll work through this in Chapter 4.)

EMBRACE DYNAMIC TEAM
STRUCTURES THAT EVOLVE AND END

Teams can become precious and important to us for good reason. When they work well, they are homes, families away from families, a center of gravity, an alliance in an unstable organization. They can give us a sense of belonging and the ease that comes with familiar ways of doing things.

All of these things are important, but we need to recognize the equal value of change in response to evolving needs. Teams must be set up to be as dynamic as the conditions themselves. Otherwise they can be working on the needs of yesterday, not what is most important today. In addition, when teams are unchanging and fixed in their ways, it can lead to complacency, rigidity, cliques, and alliances. Dynamic teams feel relevant, agile, and flexible. They feel energizing. But they have a potential downside as well. When there's too much change and uncertainty, team members find it hard to form meaningful trust and effective transparency.

The life of responsive teams means continual evolution, creation—and even dissolution—and a constant balancing of dynamism and stasis. Responsive teams are brought to life through a shared intentional purpose and then shaped by trust, respect, autonomy, continual learning, and ongoing response to current needs.

> Teams must be set up to be as dynamic as the conditions themselves. Otherwise they can be working on the needs of yesterday, not what is most important today.

People often get excited when a team is formed. There's usually a high degree of interest in being part of a new team because it feels different and relevant, there are more resources, and it potentially addresses a big problem. When teams conclude projects and/or take on new projects, these moments can be used to revisit the team purpose and members, just as the teams did in the southeastern city school district in the case study. We can create moments when people have a chance to let go of roles that no longer make sense or they are no longer best suited for, whether it's due to time constraints, passion, expertise, or a desire for new opportunities.

Responsive, dynamic teams make time to evolve the team purpose and structure to make it more relevant or to disband the team altogether in order to redistribute the time and energy back into other functions of the organization.

One example came up at a strategic plan workshop with the chief academic officer of a district in Connecticut where one of the discussion points was a review of the data and assessment team. The team had been formed a couple years earlier, and as people came and went and roles changed, somewhere along the line the purpose and meaning for the team got lost. To review and evolve the team, the exercise was pretty simple. Each person was asked first to introduce themselves by title only and then to describe what role they had on this team.

The latter part of the question was much harder for each of them. In fact, most of the people had very vague roles, like providing support and recommendations. The other thing that came out of the exercise was the fact that almost everyone in the room was on the strategy team as well as the data and assessment team. In fact, only three people were not on both teams. It turned out they no longer needed this extra team at all and the weekly meetings could cover the additional issues.

Rather than avoiding it, we should celebrate when teams get dissolved. That means that either someone was smart enough to make the important resource decision that "this is something we should no longer do" or "this is something we accomplished." If we think of organizations as living and evolving organisms, it is natural and preferable for them to adapt to a changing world, and therefore we must learn to embrace and even celebrate dynamism in our team structures.

> *Rather than avoiding it, we should celebrate when teams get dissolved.*

....

Experimenting With Teaming

Remember: Experiments are designed as trials to be tested out, iterated, studied, and broadly implemented over time. Try out and adapt the experiments on teaming to fit your role and context.

We imagine at this stage of reading you are thinking about all the teams you're currently on and the dynamics that are making some of them so effective and others so problematic. You may also be thinking about your organizational structure itself and how it may work against the very changes you're trying so hard to implement. The following suggestions will help you move from broad-stroke insights and recommendations to specific actions to enhance alignment, build trust, and practice a new level of authority—no matter what your role on a given team.

EXPERIMENT 3
Offer Feedback as Data

In their book *Words Can Shape Your Brain,* Dr. Andrew Newberg and Mark Waldman (2012) show that language shapes our behavior in powerful and unexpected ways. By choosing different words to frame and communicate our thoughts, we can instantaneously have an impact on the way we think, the way we feel, and the way others perceive us. Shifting language is a powerful way we can begin to make change—without stirring up anxiety and fostering unneeded drama. A common language can bond a team together and support a healthy team dynamic.

On a responsive team, rather than bottlenecking all work with one leader, team members enjoy the ability to use the authority that is baked into their roles, making decisions and pushing work forward as needed to fulfill the purpose. One important language shift to support this empowered team culture is offering feedback as data instead of telling someone how they should do their work. Simply put, this practice means you express your opinion as one piece of data for another person to consider, rather than the ultimate truth that they need to obey.

Rather than saying someone is wrong and you have the data to prove why, you share what you know. Instead of saying, "I've worked with Irma before and she never gets things done on time, so you need to push back your timeline," you might say, "One piece of data to consider is Irma took five weeks to get back to me last time I sent her a request, which pushed back my timeline." Thus, instead of treating your experiences as the rule of law, you are giving the person information to consider and the space to make an autonomous decision.

In a responsive team, each of us is a key source of data and perspectives. In fact, we can go so far as to say that *data* and *perspective* are interchangeable, since *perspective* can be defined as "a piece of data or fact from one specific point of view."

When we join together in a team, each person is sensing data that are only available to them in their role. It's important that we share the data we have and it's equally important to give space for these data points to be heard. (We'll have a lot more on sharing information in Chapter 5.)

Given the tendency to override, talk over, or outvote colleagues in team settings, a focus on sharing data and perspective changes the dynamic. You make it easier for others to speak up without giving rise to defensiveness. This distinction is really important. You aren't telling someone how they should do their job. You're not convincing or getting on a soapbox. Instead, you're offering a piece of perspective or data for them to consider and decide whether it serves their purpose or is not germane. And more, you're building trust as you entrust the other person to use the information you share wisely and to benefit the team and larger purpose.

Counterintuitively, we've seen that when teams begin practicing this kind of language, it allows others to consider the additional perspective to a greater degree. You are actually increasing the likelihood that it will be given fair consideration, and a more thoughtful decision is made.

Why is that? You would think that going into a meeting and saying, "Your solution won't work and I have data here to prove why" would be the strongest way to influence others. But is it? Go back to that statement and read it aloud to yourself. If you are the recipient of this piece of information, how do you feel? Defensive, protective, and probably less likely to want to integrate their perspective.

Although it might seem strange at first, couching your perspective as an additional data point or perspective and allowing the role holder to determine its usefulness leads to much more functional teams and better decisions overall.

EXPERIMENT 4
Team Meeting Protocol

Which of the following have you experienced in a meeting?

- Two loud voices drown out the rest of the voices.

- You have something to say but are unsure whether it's the right time or place.

- You wonder why you are even in this meeting.

- The meeting gets off on a side tangent and you spend the entire time talking about something that doesn't move the work forward.

- All of the above

It's true—meetings are the "necessary evil" of running an organization. We often default to meetings as our go-to way of collaborating, but what if there is a way to structure meetings for efficiency and output? Even better, what if there are other ways to collaborate?

In the lessons we talked about the importance of team practices, and there is no more important practice than coming together for a meeting. Here we introduce a meeting practice to ensure smooth and successful meetings. It will help you play by the same rules and work in a common direction. At least in the beginning, it will help to have a neutral facilitator for these meetings. As your team gets more fluent in these meetings, you can transfer facilitation to an internal team member.

This is a general team meeting protocol that can be tailored to address many subjects. You could use this as a weekly check-in to enhance transparency and move the work forward. You could also use this to process bigger-ticket issues, make decisions, and address team structures and roles.

1. **Check in.** Each person has a chance to call out what has their attention and get present in the meeting. Each person speaks in turn.

2. **Revisit previous action items (as needed).** The facilitator asks, "Did you complete the action items from the last meeting?" Each person in turn goes around and says "yes" or "not yet" with no further discussion. If a person wants to talk more about it, or if someone wants to inquire about a "not yet," they can bring it up as an agenda item in the following section.

3. **Build the agenda "on the fly."** Anyone can speak up with an agenda item. No discussion needed, just two or three words to hold a place on the agenda. Everyone can speak. The facilitator captures the agenda on a public medium.

4. **Open an agenda item**. Start with agenda item one. The facilitator asks the agenda item owner "What do you need?" and allows the agenda item owner to set the tone. The person may be looking for feedback, a discussion, or simply to share an FYI with the group. The facilitator and the agenda item owner talk.

5. **Process agenda item**. The owner opens discussion as needed to resolve the item. Anyone can talk as needed to process the agenda item. The facilitator should monitor the discussion. If the discussion seems to be veering into other topics, the facilitator can redirect by asking the agenda item owner, "Are you getting what you need?" or the person speaking can be asked to hold their comments and add a separate agenda item once this one is closed out. A note taker should capture any action items that surface during processing with clear ownership over each action.

6. **Close the agenda item**. The facilitator reads out loud any captured action items and asks agenda item holder, "Did you get what you needed?" When the person says "yes," check off the agenda item and move to the next item. The facilitator and the agenda owner talk.

7. **Repeat steps 4–6 for each agenda item**. Being mindful of time, the goal is to get to all agenda items in the allotted time.

8. **Check out**. Share a reflection or learning from the meeting. Each person speaks in turn.

A few notes about this process:

- It's obvious given the notes above that the facilitator has a key role in getting this practice off to a good start. Identify a strong, neutral facilitator who isn't afraid to hold the space firmly and is able to cut off conversation when needed.

- If feasible, a note taker or someone in the secretary role can support the facilitator by capturing any action items that surface during processing of the agenda. This role also acts as a check and balance to the role of team steward, which we'll see in Chapter 3. The team steward is then free to focus their energy on the team as a whole and to leverage their expertise, but is given healthy boundaries within the structure of this protocol so they aren't interrupting or usurping conversation and the needs and ideas of team members.

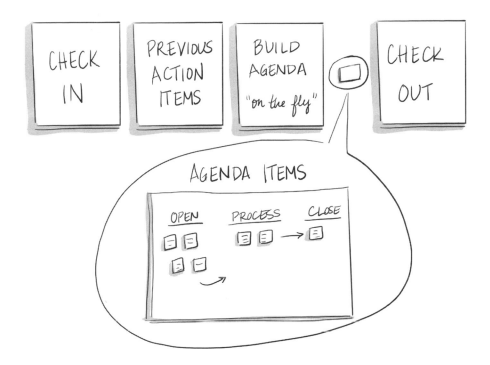

- The check-in and check-out are simple but effective bookends to get people present in the meeting and to extract learning on their way out.

- The "on the fly" agenda is important because everyone has the opportunity to bring up topics they need to resolve to move their work forward. Also, because the agenda is made on the spot, it's impossible for people to come in with predetermined biases and opinions on any topic. The name of the game is to get what you need from the group and move on.

- Finally, meetings do not have to be the default way to collaborate. With endless technological options, there are many good ways to come together as a team and collaborate. Even making a proposal via e-mail for quick decisions can work—try putting forth a proposal with this language: "Here is background information and my proposal. If you have any clarifying questions, reactions, or concerns, please respond to me within seventy-two hours. If I don't hear from you, then I will move forward." Other, more advanced tools for real-time chat or shared documents can help you solve a problem and get some feedback without having to call a meeting. The bottom line is getting smart about working together so that you can make the most progress toward your purpose.

Teaming Is Working When . . .

Many people have a natural desire to work in teams, which is a positive impulse that can be harnessed to create thriving school cultures and outcomes. In the field of education, where most staff began their careers in classrooms and teacher teams, there is a wealth of experience to draw on. The challenge is to overcome the problems that are working against the very enthusiasm and creativity we all want.

Teaming is working when . . .

There's a greater sense of being alive. Teams will feel dynamic and relevant. It won't feel like you are wasting your time in meetings. It won't feel like you are on a team that isn't relevant anymore. You will see teams grow and shrink, come and go—like a living organism, teams will expand and contract as needed instead of becoming hollow political bodies that are around just for legacy's sake. It will feel like you are connected to the rest of the organization and able to access the information you need to move work forward. You will be able to get things done faster, with less reliance on approval from others.

Teams and organizations have a clear and motivating purpose. Team purpose will be clear; it will align to meaningful accountabilities that are owned by members of your team. You can determine quickly who the one person is that is accountable for the work, and when asked, they confirm the same.

Everyone is continuously evolving, improving, and aiming higher. Instead of relying on a manager or leader to resolve problems and make decisions in your work, an increased focus on distributed authority will support people to take ownership over their work and push their own development.

CHAPTER 3

Managing Roles

Define the Work Before You Define the People

Think about all the different roles we play in life, as spouses and partners, as friends and colleagues, as coaches of our kids' teams and volunteers in the community. Yet in our work, a different notion has been baked into our identities. We've come to believe that we *are* our role or title—that we're bosses, supervisors, senior teachers, specialists, or whatever label and title has been given to us.

These labels can be important markers of our experience (time invested) and expertise (skills gained). But they don't necessarily equate to all the roles we play each day—the planner, advisor, teacher, decision maker, and communicator. Our job descriptions become fallbacks and crutches. Where else would the sentiment "not my job"—or "that's not *your* job"—come from? Rather than being able to step into our different roles with clarity and purpose, our titles become a uniform that we can't take off.

> *Rather than being able to step into our different roles with clarity and purpose, our titles become a uniform that we can't take off.*

In fact, all of us play multiple roles at work. In an environment where responsive teams are the leading drivers of an organization's purpose, the roles we play will vary by the needs and goals of each team we're part of. We may play a leading, supporting, facilitating, or expert role depending on the project and circumstances. When we think about roles, and not just titles and job descriptions, we get a powerful tool for clarifying the work we're doing, the roles of our colleagues, as well as our personal purpose as it aligns with the organization.

 ## The Problem

Among educators there is a palpable, driving purpose to improve student outcomes. This laser focus is why people enter the field in the first place. Depending on your position, you likely have a narrower purpose that supports this big, broad ambitious vision.

- A policymaker's purpose is to set forth policies that promote improvement in student outcomes.

- A recruiter's purpose is to acquire talent that is skilled and interested in the field of education.

- A philanthropist's purpose is to catalyze resources and effort for a school or school district.

Yet with all of these smart, purpose-driven people working on improving student outcomes, why is it so hard to see dramatic change? Even when the desire is there, it's a challenge to organize a bunch of ambitious, committed, emotional, caring, imperfect human beings into actual roles to get the work done.

The "getting the work done" part of the equation is often stymied by our legacy approach of defining jobs and responsibilities. In the age of the craftsperson, a shop owner and maybe one or two helpers did every stage and all aspects of the work. A baker purchased supplies, developed recipes or used those handed down, prepared and baked the dough, opened the store, served customers, collected money, paid bills, and cleaned up every day. A violinmaker purchased wood and other supplies, developed tools and unique designs, painstakingly built the instrument, solicited commissions, sold the finished item, and developed their brand through relationships with musicians, prominent figures, mentors, and fellow craftspeople. The craftsperson cared about the whole experience of their work from start to end, including engaging with and responding to customers who enjoyed the fruits of their labor.

As we moved from a craftsperson age to an industrial age, factories with specialized roles allowed for the uniform creation of projects, greater speed and efficiency, and the rise of management as a specific skill. Without belaboring a history of work and labor, the relevant point for today is that static, hierarchical job descriptions and rigid definitions of the industrial age are getting in our way.

We can't go back to the craftsperson era, yet we're in a period with a renewed desire for personalized and meaningful experiences. We want those experiences, services, and products to be fast, ubiquitous, afford-

> *Static, hierarchical job descriptions and rigid definitions of the industrial age are getting in our way.*

able, and more equitable. And as leaders and workers in this new digital age, we also want to move beyond the transactional role of the industrial age assembly-line laborer into roles with personal purpose. Empowered by technology doing so much of the rote work, we want to bring our whole selves to our work. It's that sense of individual purpose—paired with team clarity and alignment—that fosters success and impact.

Just think of the Starbucks barista. The person who tends the espresso machine is both a coffee maker and a welcoming experience maker, a voice for the company and a connection builder.

We need to let go of fixed descriptions of our work and move toward a focus on teams made up of continually evolving roles.

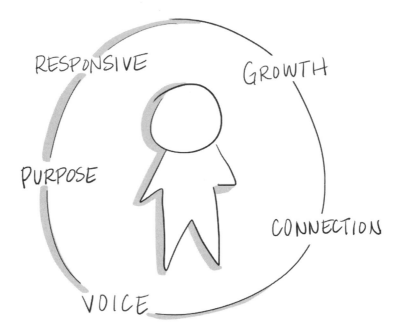

RESPONSIVE GROWTH

PURPOSE

CONNECTION

VOICE

JOB DESCRIPTIONS GET IN THE WAY

When was the last time you referenced your job description to determine what you should be doing on a given day? You probably haven't referenced it since the day you were hired because the day you started, that job description was out of date—a relic in a fast-paced and changing environment.

Though we're hired for a job description, most of our work isn't *on* our description—it's *for* the constantly evolving teams we're on. That's the real work we're accountable for.

That's why in our schools and school districts, where needs and conditions are continuously changing, job descriptions create gaps. All of us have encountered situations where projects failed because the work was divided into artificial silos, communications were broken, and hand-offs were poor. We've also been involved in projects that took too long to get off the ground because it wasn't clear who should own the project since it didn't neatly fall under someone's job description. There are also times where someone is willing to lead a project but isn't able to fully own it because someone else has formal "domain control."

Imagine a coach putting together a basketball team without each player being very clear about the position and roles they play. Even if you have the best players, the outcomes can be miserable. An example of this might look like the U.S. Olympic basketball team that played in the 2004 Athens games and suffered an upset loss to Argentina. The U.S. team was stud-

> *We've been involved in projects that took too long to get off the ground because it wasn't clear who should own the project since it didn't neatly fall under someone's job description.*

ded with amazing players (LeBron James, Dwyane Wade, Carmelo Anthony, Tim Duncan, to name a few), but it was imbalanced and there was too much overlap in certain positions. They weren't able to come together as a cohesive unit of distinct roles.

Job descriptions are often generic and broad, written to capture all the current work and all the potential future work in nonspecific terms in order to cover the bases for any and all eventualities. But that means there's very little clarity about who is responsible for what—who is accountable.

Take a look at these three job descriptions at a school district—director of administrative services, director of teaching and learning, and elementary principal—and consider these questions:

- Who is accountable for developing district and school leaders?

- Which areas do each of these positions focus on in developing and coaching district and school leaders?

- Who reviews and selects curriculum and instructional resources?

Among just these three positions, accountabilities related to strategy and community engagement, finances, curriculum, professional development, and administration all overlap. Notice the fuzziness around who is accountable for coaching and development across the organization or for reviewing and selecting curriculum and instructional resources. This lack of clarity can lead to a few impacts:

- No one takes responsibility and everyone waits for someone else to push the project forward.

- Grandstanding, tiptoeing, avoiding, and passive-aggressive behavior all to placate real or imagined hierarchies, loyalties, and politics.

Areas of Responsibility for Three Typical Job Descriptions in a School District

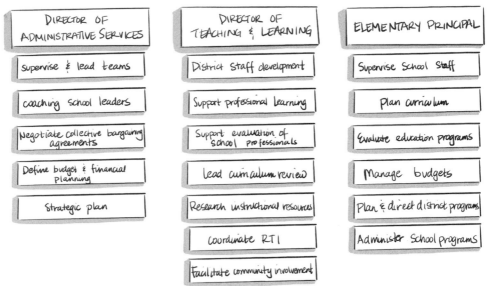

- Many meetings and discussions feel like "one step forward and two steps back" as everyone wants to "play nice" and include everyone in the process.

- Hours are wasted talking in circles and developing consensus because everyone believes they have a role in the decision.

- Stopgap decisions are made to let everyone feel like progress is being made.

School leaders and teachers will chalk up this confusion to ineptitude and indecision. But more often than not, the lack of clear roles and purpose is a root cause of ineffective teams. We can fool ourselves into thinking everything is covered because multiple people are involved so "someone must be handling it." However, we know that when accountabilities are aligned to multiple people, it doesn't get done.

ROLE OVERWHELM (AND UNDERWHELM)

A focus on job descriptions and hierarchies not only gets in the way of clarifying our roles; it can also reinforce land grabs, as we saw in Chapter 2, contributing to feelings of being besieged by work if you are a duke of one of the metaphoric fiefdoms or, alternately, underutilized and uninvolved if you're one of the serfs.

Too often we see one person on a team doing 80 percent of the work. The more this one person does, the less the others do. Team members are present for meetings and offer free advice, but they provide little mindshare after the meeting and no ownership of the overall goals. It's usually not about lack of interest but about lack of clarity of their role. Their job descriptions might indicate they belong at the meeting, but the team hasn't defined what their role should be once they get there.

School organizations can become highly dysfunctional when lack of clarity around roles creates unhealthy competition and jockeying for position. More time can be spent fighting individual battles for control and influence than on the work itself.

An instructional coaching team at a southeastern school district was struggling with an expanding list of assignments, and they'd hit a wall in being able to deliver work successfully. When the team was asked what services they provided to individual schools, their initial descriptions were things like "providing support," "connecting the dots," and "bringing in additional resources if possible."

> *School organizations can become highly dysfunctional when lack of clarity around roles creates unhealthy competition and jockeying for position.*

When they were pushed to provide more specifics, they couldn't describe what value and specific roles they provided. Digging into the history of the team, they realized that over time their roles had become murky. This team had picked up the work other leaders in the district didn't want because the work had to get done. The team had become a catchall for all the things the district office didn't know what to do with. The team was feeling more and more overwhelmed at the same time they were feeling less and less effective. Instead of being proud of their efforts to empower schools and help teachers succeed, they were skimming the surface of what would truly improve instruction.

A typical principal's job description may have the following areas of work: instructional leadership, program planning, school management, community relations, business management, and professional development. Each of these focus areas might have ten to twenty specific accountabilities. To close out a five-page job description, there might be the "bonus" statement under a heading Knowledge and Abilities: "To perform the responsibilities as previously outlined." (By the way, that's not meant to be funny!)

Numerous discussions with principals across the country reveal that many of them experience tremendous pressure and have a sense they are being unsuccessful because of complete exhaustion and working twelve-hour days attempting to carry out everything on their plate.

There must be a more strategic way to divide and share the work. With role clarity, we can begin to practice a transparent approach regarding our purpose and priorities. Each person can be confident in taking authority for their roles and in how they fit into the bigger picture. We can transparently adjust our role to fit the needs and purpose of the teams we're part of, and we can work with our colleagues and other teams to make sure the purpose of the work is clear—and necessary. It's possible to have less confusion and overwhelm, more confidence and effectiveness, and more satisfaction at every level of the organization.

 ## The New Rule

Define the Work Before You Define the People

When we apply the New Rule *define the work before you define the people*, we mean that as organizations take on new streams of work or projects, the first step is to clearly articulate the purpose of the work and the work that needs to be done to fulfill that purpose. Only then, after there's a basic picture of where we want to go, can we ask who is best able to do it and what skills and roles are missing.

Think about a group of people learning to play a new board game. It might go something like this: One person opens up the game and starts taking out the pieces. Another person might grab the instructions and begin reading the objectives and basic rules, calling attention to key pieces of information needed to proceed in setting up the game. One or two people might start sorting all the pieces and dabble with setting up the board, while another person organizes the cards or player pieces. Once the game gets under way, people are playing together but also taking on individual roles like Banker or Rule Interpreter.

Let's say your school district just won a significant federal grant of $20 million to transform teaching and learning across the district over the next three years. The plan for the project sets the big picture direction, but who should lead the work? The director of administrative services? The director of teaching and learning? An outside consultant brought in to organize and kick off the project?

Well, what if we first asked what work needed to be done to achieve the purpose: "Transform teaching and learning across the district over the next three years." The work may include the following:

- designing new instructional practices and school models that focus on differentiated small-group instruction

- training a third of the teachers each year on instructional strategies like blended learning or project-based learning

- curating digital resources and tools to enhance the instructional experience for all students and offer choices to each school site

Once you have this starting point for the roles and accountabilities, then you can recruit the people with the right skills to fulfill them. The leadership team might create a new team to drive the initiative, or they might review their existing teams to see if they have the right people to drive the different aspects of the project. That's the crux of the New Rule to *define the work before you define the people.*

Most people will have several active roles at a given time, each with its distinct purpose and scope. We can think of each person being the "steward" of their multiple roles. In this way, we are responsible for our roles and our accountabilities—and our confusions and conflicts when they surely arrive. We are stewards of how we manage our work, get the support we need, and engage with team members and coordinate, as needed, with other teams.

What happens when we approach roles this way?

- Because the work has been defined clearly, the people assigned to these roles have much more clarity about what they need to be working on and where they have authority and decision-making power.

- Each person will feel more valued because what they do is more effective and meaningful.

- People in roles feel like they are getting more done, because each action they take will have more precision. We talk about precision in our actions because people can be more efficient and effective with their accountabilities and deliverables when we can be precise with what they need to do.

- Workloads vary for team members so people aren't trying to expend equal effort in each of their roles since each role will require a different level of effort.

- People are able to step in and out of roles as the needs of the organization, team, and individuals evolve.

- There are fewer gaps and less confusion because roles are transparent and understood within and across teams.

If you begin to think about roles as organic cells that come alive, merge, evolve, or die off, you will get a better sense of what roles

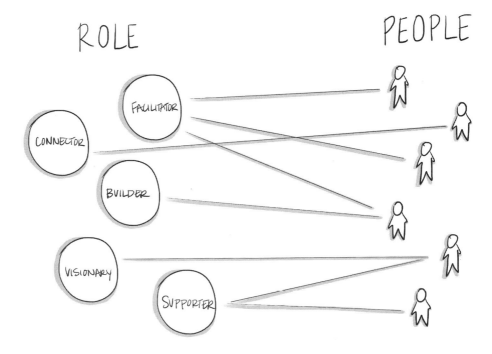

look like in a responsive organization. These roles will evolve over time to best fulfill the purpose. Roles aren't conflated with individuals or names; they exist independently for their needed skills, experiences, or perspectives. Additionally, with a framework of responsive roles, people can have multiple roles on multiple teams across the organization because multiple projects are going on.

> *We are stewards of how we manage our work, get the support we need, and engage with team members and coordinate, as needed, with other teams.*

Case Study: Implementing a Big Vision by Tapping an Internal Leader

A school district with approximately 7,300 students is located outside a large city. Its demographics are similar to many other districts in the country: 73 percent of its students qualify for free or reduced-price lunch, 80 percent belong to minority groups, and 20 percent are English language learners.

The superintendent observed that the number of students living in poverty grew from 54 percent in 2004 to 76 percent in 2011. Students in his district had parents who worked at night, and some lived in shelters. In these circumstances, he knew that doubling down on surface changes, such as giving students more homework as a strategy to improve learning, was a strategy for failure. Looking for a new way, the district leadership envisioned an approach that responded to the actual needs of their families and lives, which included 50 percent unemployment due to lack of education and few opportunities for advancement.

The district leadership focused on a vision for academic success by changing the way the district served the community. As they understood it, either they could continue down a path of low graduation rates and long-term poverty or they could apply for a federal grant to change the trajectory of their community. They came up with a simple, powerful purpose: Eliminate the look and feel of poverty.

In December 2012, the district won the grant. The approach the district chose to take started with the following:

- Personalized learning for every child.
- Create welcoming and friendly classrooms with learning pods.
- Have large open green spaces.
- Offer competitive athletic facilities.

The instructional elements of the plan included the following:

- Reinvent professional development for new blended learning strategies.
- Implement master classes for accelerating students.
- Provide two-year kindergarten for students starting behind.
- Develop and implement a mid-year intervention program.
- Use a data analytics strategy.

With all of this system-level change, you would think that a large committee would have been formed, headed by a proven and familiar person in the district, or a new chief would have been named to lead the project. But that's not what happened.

No one expected the superintendent to manage the project. But then why didn't they tap Roger, the assistant superintendent of instruction, to take it on? Following the New Rule to *define the work before you define the people,* several opportunities presented themselves.

First, the district cabinet decided the assistant superintendent had other priorities and smartly decided against bolting on another project. Second, instead of hiring another person to project manage this work and figure it out, they focused on understanding the scope of the work that needed to be done internally and tapping someone who would be ready and passionate about the opportunity. We have observed that districts are notorious for outsourcing key projects due to limited capacity, but they then lose all that knowledge and experience when the outside group moves on. Third, they believed it would be harder and slower to get buy-in from their high schools, so they decided to start the initial work in the elementary schools. Since Roger's focus area was high school, it made sense to have someone who worked in elementary schools.

All that effort and clarity ultimately led the district to tap Ann, the principal of one of the district's elementary schools, to project manage this work. Although the superintendent developed the vision and overall strategy, he believed the success of the project would be achieved through the schools and the teachers. Their rate of adoption would be critical to the execution of this project.

Ann jumped at the opportunity and we believe she excelled in her role because she was close to the ground (the classrooms). Separating out the work to be done from names of people that came to mind created the opportunity for a new person to take on the new effort, expanding leadership capacity. In addition, we posit that implementing the New Rule to *define the work before you define the people* helped create a culture where other people didn't feel their role was being diminished when someone else took on a new role. Everyone knew that new work would be assigned according to skill, availability, passion, and growth and not according to status or job titles.

There were added benefits, too. For example, when staff at the elementary schools had some down time, they squeezed in time for their Laundry Project, which meant collecting clothes left around the schools and washing them so children who had less would be able to wear clean, warm clothes. In a limited capacity, Ann continued on the Laundry Project team, provided her helping hand, and suggested additional volunteers or highlighted shared problems or gaps she noticed in her school rounds.

We believe that assigning people to roles versus assigning favorites and leaders according to titles to a project allows organizations to manage work based on two critical success criteria.

1. *Interest and passion.* Instead of denying people opportunity because it's not in their title, you can factor their interest into who is assigned.

2. *Experience or skills.* Having prior knowledge or experience makes getting started and not making common mistakes more likely. While experience can be an important factor, the skills to discover and process information can be even more powerful.

In the case of this district team, Ann didn't have the weight of the whole project on her shoulders. Her role was defined as the team steward, the person who makes sure the work gets done. Her authority and accountabilities were set around making sure the project maintained its momentum. This is very different than trying to make or be a part of every decision. In fact, her experience with a defined and limited mandate made it easier for her to identify and allow other roles to take leadership in their arenas, though there were snags and lessons along the way.

We observed two factors played into the success of this team. First, like a highly functioning basketball team, everyone was clear about their roles. Each person was crystal clear on what they needed to get done in order to continue to move the ball forward. They understood why it was important to *define the work before you define the people*. Sometimes a team member played a bigger part in the work, and other times their role would be removed as the work changed.

Second, as the team steward, Ann made sure she facilitated the conversations where individual roles, expectations, or accountabilities were unclear. The focus on clear roles ensured that as new situations arose work would be assigned to the appropriate person. Everyone got used to shifting and new responsibilities, which helped minimize internal roadblocks that might have gotten in the way of the bigger purpose.

Lessons

As we can see with the case study, big changes are possible, and many of us probably have more of the talent and resources we need right in front of us. When we define the work before we define the people, the clarity of roles and accountabilities makes the work more efficient and less taxing. It also becomes less political as there is transparency in expectations and everyone has a voice and a defined role to play. When we steward our own multiple roles and observe others doing the same, we begin to experience a much more flexible idea of leadership, expertise, and value.

> *When we steward our own multiple roles and observe others doing the same, we begin to experience a much more flexible idea of leadership, expertise, and value.*

A set of lessons can give you a conceptual framework to start you on the path to this new way of thinking and acting. And we'll follow those with some concrete how-tos to get you started. Here are the cornerstone lessons for approaching our work as stewards of our multiple roles:

- Put a role's purpose before politics.

- Separate roles for personal clarity and smarter decisions.

- Value each voice as a human sensor.

PUT A ROLE'S PURPOSE BEFORE POLITICS

When we jump to identifying team members (no matter how high-potential or skilled they are) before explicitly defining the work to be done, we actually interfere with successful team building. Here's why:

1. We tend to adjust our expectations to the person we think will be able to fulfill the role rather than defining what true success would look like and getting creative about who can fill that role.

2. Discussions about who should do what are inherently personal and can be political. When drafting an internal team for

a high-stakes project, the discussion usually focuses on which senior-level staff member we should expect to steward the work. The merits of each person are discussed, and there is much back-and-forth about who would make the best fit. If we stop focusing on the individuals and focus on creating a really robust role, as we believe was the case with Ann in the case study, then it is much easier to consider who would be the best person to fulfill the role and accountabilities.

Sometimes it turns out that one role needs to be divided into two, or a stream of work belongs somewhere else. Over and over, we see that the practice of defining the work first helps people get out of the morass of personal attributes and political positions and quickly moves the focus to the work that needs to be done.

3. We tend to reach for the same "superstars" to take leading roles, especially when the work isn't clearly defined. Defining the work first levels the playing field for people to understand the needs and pitch themselves for new roles and projects.

The funny thing is that when you *define the work before you define the people,* it is actually good for people. A focus on roles, accountabilities, and explicitness doesn't have to be soulless. The confidence that comes with filling a clear role actually empowers people to speak up with authority for the roles they fill.

SEPARATE ROLES FOR PERSONAL CLARITY AND SMARTER DECISIONS

No matter what your job description, it's likely you already fill more than one role. How do you know? Make a mental (or better yet, a physical) note of the things that are expected of you. Do some of these expectations serve different purposes? Can you make groupings of your accountabilities based on similar purpose? Then you fill multiple roles.

> The funny thing is that when you define the work before you define the people, it is actually good for people.

For example, the job of office manager might have several roles across different teams. At the Education

Elements offices, the office manager plays a role on the teams for employee health and happiness, administration, employee on-boarding, and the annual summit. For each role on the different teams, she has different degrees of decision-making authority. In any of these roles, it's also easy to imagine moving different people into them because the accountabilities are specific to the work and not comingled with an individual job description.

David Rose is the former deputy chief of education technology and library programs at District of Columbia Public Schools. Not only does David's team play a role on the information technology team, they also participate in roles on curriculum teams with specific accountabilities to decide on technologies to support the goals of the curriculum department. His team also participates in advisory roles on the professional development, academic chiefs, alternative programs, and budget teams. They kept their roles and accountabilities for each team on a public document that each of them could readily access and update when workload conflicts arose. They knew what their purpose was on the team and where their authority lay (e.g., advising, approving, providing general knowledge). This clarity of purpose and roles enhanced the effectiveness of everyone on the team.

In David's case, as the head of a department in high demand, he felt the clarity of his role on each specific team allowed him to be more effective with his time and expertise. On teams where he had a decision-making role, he always felt he had the authority to move forward on things he needed to advance without having to get buy-in from everyone else because his role made it clear that he had the ultimate authority to move work forward. At the same time, when he was supporting other teams in an advisory role, he didn't feel like they had to integrate his ideas into every decision, nor did he need to agree with every decision. As long as there was clarity of roles, he was assured that someone had the clear authority to move work forward to fulfill their purpose.

For his book *Reinventing Organizations,* Frederic Laloux (2014) studied organizations that embody this shift. He writes, "Thinking in terms of granular roles instead of pre-defined jobs creates great fluidity and adaptability." To make the

> *To make the transition to a more responsive model of stewardship of multiple roles, think of each person managing an ever-evolving set of roles.*

transition to a more responsive model of stewardship of multiple roles, think of each person managing an ever-evolving set of roles that, as Laloux describes, "they pick up based on their interests and talents and the needs of the organization" (pp. 258–259).

To help capture the essence of your roles, you can think about a few things:

- Which of your roles require clear decision-making authority?

- Which of your roles have more of a supporting, expert, or experience part for you to play?

- Do you see places to rethink your roles, resign from or reassign your role, or take on more?

> *Role clarity helps break through hierarchy because we're no longer measured by our height on a hierarchy but on our effectiveness in fulfilling the purpose of our role.*

Rather than staying stuck in the land-grab mentality we discussed in Chapter 2, the shift to being stewards of our responsive, evolving roles encourages everyone to quickly assess the skills and bandwidth needed to fulfill a role and possibly identify a better home for the work. Removing one role, among many, can feel like less of a blow than giving up your whole position and title.

Role clarity helps break through hierarchy because we're no longer measured by our height on a hierarchy but on our effectiveness in fulfilling the purpose of our role, and each of us can work on getting more comfortable holding multiple roles with different levels of responsibility.

At Zappos, the innovative shoe retailer, CEO Tony Hsieh has held leadership roles at the highest levels as well as support roles within a customer service team. While it might be easy for Tony to walk into to the customer service circle with the attitude of "I'm the CEO and I can veto any decision," his role on that team limits his authority to providing advice. As you might imagine, being able to move from one team to another without bringing the authority of other roles can be challenging. It's like wearing two separate hats. It can sometimes help to visualize it that way, for example, "I'm taking off my special projects lead hat and putting on my

IT support hat." With ongoing practice and holding each other accountable, you can strengthen this skill over time.

Although the types of roles will vary and be content specific, here are a few archetypes of the basic roles or role categories that might show up on your teams:

- *Team steward*—brings clarity to mission and purpose, accesses the right funding and resources for the work, and surfaces important updates, measures, and reports to move the work forward

- *Content experts*—have knowledge and experience to do the work

- *Observers and advisors*—provide data points and advice as representatives of related teams and stakeholders, but no authority for decisions of the team

- *Secretary*—keeps a record of roles, takes notes, and reports out on action items

VALUE EACH VOICE AS A HUMAN SENSOR

With all this focus on roles, we want to call out that the most important factor in responsive organizations is the people. It's people stewarding their roles that drives work forward. In a responsive organization, filling a role comes with great autonomy and responsibility.

As people take on the mantle of their roles, they become valuable human sensors for the role they fill. If *valuable human sensor* sounds like a touchy-feely term, that's because it is! Responsive organizations know that to maximize the impact of the organization, every person must be empowered to leverage their perspective for the greater purpose. This is an important shift. It honors *all* voices, not just those who are privileged by seniority, formal authority, or connections.

> Every person must be empowered to leverage their perspective for the greater purpose. This is an important shift. It honors all voices, not just those who are privileged by seniority, formal authority, or connections.

As an analogy, think of the warning lights in your car. Have you ever had the light come on and you look at the oil gauge, check your windshield wiper fluid and gas, and everything looks okay and the car was recently serviced? Given all the evidence, you might be tempted to ignore the sensor and keep driving. Most of us can ignore the light—sometimes for months. And then you run out of gas on the side of the road because it turns out that your gas cap was leaking.

Ultimately, each sensor has unique and valuable data. It's a mistake to assume that if other sensors aren't reporting anything, nothing is wrong. The impact of ignoring valuable human sensors shouldn't be seen just from an organizational risk perspective, but also from a human perspective, because what happens when someone's sensor gets ignored over and over again? Frustrations and tensions build and people shut down and disengage from their work.

When we regard each person as someone with unique and valuable data for their roles, we change the culture and each person's engagement with their work and roles. We allow organizations to harness diversity of thought. People experience the authority of each of their multiple roles. They know the "data" from their experience and expertise matters. They know their feelings and reactions offer a unique lens and awareness. Whether a role is as a team leader keeping a whole project on track or as an expert on a particular issue, people sense their value to the larger purpose. It creates fluidity and breaks down artificial hierarchies. We're all valuable human sensors, and it's all valuable information to be used in the best way to move the work forward.

· ·

EXPERIMENTS

Experimenting With Managing Roles

Remember: Experiments are designed as trials to be tested out, iterated, studied, and broadly implemented over time. Try out and adapt the experiments on managing roles to fit your role and context.

Moving from a focus on titles and traditional job descriptions to a framework of roles and accountabilities is an important shift for responsive organizations. The concept of roles—and role stewardship—gives us a powerful tool for clarifying the work we're doing and helps us align our personal purpose with the organization's. Well-conceived roles anchor our teams, can help break down artificial silos, and lead to collaboration that works. Play with the following experiments to get started.

EXPERIMENT 5

Role Mapping

In an ideal world, a new team always begins with a clear purpose and defined roles. But you might be months or years into working with a team when you realize your roles are not clear or what you thought was clear is a big muddle of different, and sometimes clashing, expectations.

For example, we worked with a CEO who saw herself as a "culture architect" as well as a "professor whose purpose was to bring in external perspective and vision," while the rest of the leadership team felt they needed something very different from her. They saw her playing the role of "strategic vision and priority setting." Exposing this disparity was a great jumping-off point to realign the team's roles and accountabilities to achieve their desired purpose.

When roles aren't clear, it impacts team dynamics. If we don't see someone living up to the implicit accountabilities we have for their role, we lose trust in them—even if they never knew it was an expectation to begin with.

When we follow the New Rule to *define the work before you define the people,* the goal is to evolve the team toward clarity so a culture of autonomy, explicit authority, and trust can be built. It lessens the need to jockey for power and recognition when each person has clarity around their work and needed contribution.

This role-mapping activity results in a starting structure for each team you are on. It's important to emphasize *starting* because as a team's work evolves, so should its structure. In this activity you will create a workable structure that captures the ongoing activities of today. No need to get creative. Capture the facts to establish a foundation for your team, which you'll revisit over time. If you are on more than one team, you can do this activity with each team that you're on. We recommend starting with the team that captures most of your time and energy.

1. **Individual work**. Take a stab at breaking your work into roles. Ask yourself:

   What is expected of me?

   Take some time to generate a list. As you write, try to sort the expectations into related work buckets. For example if you are in human resources, all the expectations related to recruiting might be in one bucket, all the expectations related to onboarding in another, and so on. Use your best judgment to create these buckets—there are no right or wrong answers. The goal is just to create a document that begins to capture all of your roles. When you're done you'll have a document that looks something like this:

   Recruiting Role
   - reaching out to applicants
   - scheduling interview days

   Onboarding Role
   - sending onboarding e-mail with new hire paperwork
   - connecting new hires with IT to obtain supplies

2. **Group work**. Have each person bring their brainstorm to a meeting. Pass these around or share on a platform (such as Google Docs) to give everyone a chance to read through everyone's roles. Pose the question:

   What additional or different expectations do you have for these roles?

   Invite all team members to read each other's roles and add their own expectations to the document, and fill in any missing accountabilities or roles.

   The question of how specific you should get with expectations is a common challenge, and there is no one-size-fits-all answer. One of the underlying principles of responsive organizations is allowing authority to reside with the roles closest to the work. In this spirit, accountabilities should allow sufficient room for the role holder to decide how to best energize the accountability and not overly dictate exactly how the role needs to be executed.

   If starting with general accountabilities worries you, keep in mind that over time you can always adjust accountabilities and make them more specific as needed. For example, if you started by articulating an accountability for a family communication role as "communicating regularly with parents" and over time you realize that it's helpful to include more specifics to better help others understand your work, you could update the accountability to read, "leveraging current mailing list technology to send out monthly parent updates with news and upcoming events."

   As with most features of responsive organizations, there isn't a hard-and-fast rule here—you must scale the amount of structure to meet the needs of the work and continue to refine and evolve that structure over time.

3. **Group reflection**. Once the team has had an opportunity to add to each other's ideas, open the floor to discussion. Use this question to spur reflection:

   What discrepancies, surprises, or questions surfaced as you reflected on this activity?

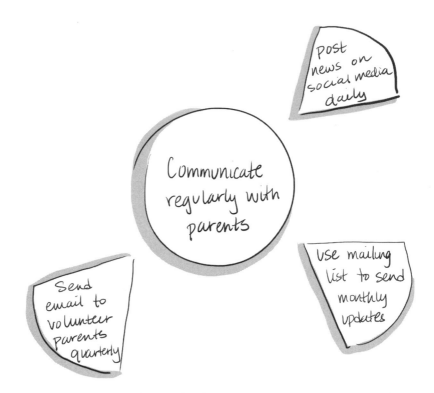

4. **Individual work**. Using the feedback provided, allow team members an opportunity to leave the table and refine their roles individually. As you refine your role, ask yourself:

Is my work captured in these roles?

What is the purpose of each of my roles?

Remember from Chapter 2 that a purpose describes the aim you wish to achieve for that role. Not only does the purpose help define the identity of the role, but also a clear purpose helps establish clear role authority, which is essential. At the end you will have a list of roles that looks like this:

Recruiting

Purpose: Prospective employees are connected with opportunities and communicated with in a way that builds positive relationships with the district.

- reaching out to applicants
- scheduling interview days

Onboarding

Purpose: A smooth and seamless onboarding experience introduces new hires to the positive team culture of our district.

- sending onboarding e-mail with new hire paperwork

- connecting new hires with IT to obtain supplies

5. **Regular group review.** Once team members have captured sufficient starting roles, keep them as team records. Revisit these records monthly. Ask these review questions:

Is there anything we need to add? Is there something we want to start doing?

Is there anything we need to get rid of? Is there something we want to stop doing?

Is there anything we need to update for clarity's sake?

This starting structure provides structural clarity that teams need, and the process of evolving it on a regular basis helps encourage the agility that teams desire.

EXPERIMENT 6

The One-Question Technique

One of the benefits of defining work by first defining roles is that it helps clarify the accountabilities and authority each person has. Rather than needing the group to labor over consensus for every decision, we can clearly identify which role has the authority to move work forward and empower that person to take charge. In fact, when you notice a discussion getting bogged down and off track, try jumping in and asking this one question:

Which role has the authority to make this decision?

This simple question refocuses the discussion on the role holders who are stewards of that particular issue and quiets unnecessary back-and-forth from people who are tangential to the issue.

EXPERIMENT 7

Guidelines for Being an Effective Sensor

To step into the authority of your roles, you need to embrace four key actions:

1. *Proactively steward your roles*. You are expected to steward your roles by continuously taking action that will move your work forward. This means considering what actions you can take to fulfill your accountabilities and proactively taking those actions without needing someone to tell you to do it.

2. *Surface tensions.* As we discussed in Chapter 2, whether you call it tension, frustration, friction, or strain, the fact remains that it's inevitable. Even when we think about it this way, it's still easier to ignore these feelings than to surface them. But if you ignore tension, you may be missing an opportunity to evolve the organization in a positive direction. In this sense, it's your role's sacred duty to surface tension and try to resolve it. When you step into the authority of your role, you can't rely on someone else to bring up issues on your behalf; you have to be in charge of that. Even if it feels like you're too junior to bring up certain types of concerns, you have to trust that you have a unique perspective from your role that could be useful. Experiment 9: Protocol for a Starting Proposal (in Chapter 4) offers steps you can take to more formally surface tensions.

3. *Offer data.* You need to use your unique perspective to offer feedback and data that can help other roles take informed actions. Sharing key data and information from your role keeps others informed and provides unique insight to inform next steps. As we saw in Chapter 2, sharing your information as data can go a long way toward reducing resistance and defensiveness.

4. *Prioritize.* Holding a role doesn't mean you will be able to execute 100 percent of your accountabilities and tasks 100 percent the time. In all healthy, growing organizations, there will be more work to do than time to do it given limited resources. This is a natural tension and one that will never go away. This means you have to consider all your roles and make decisions about which roles to prioritize in a given moment in order to have the most impact in moving the

organization forward. If significant decisions need to be made that will affect your team members yet it's unclear who should be making these decisions or it creates more issues, this is a sign that a team's roles and accountabilities need attention or calibration.

Starting with just one of these suggestions can begin an important shift with the potential to unleash the power of all the roles in the organization.

....

Managing Roles Is Working When . . .

As individuals within organizations begin to define their own multiple roles, they have a personal wake-up call. On the one hand, it can be overwhelming to recognize how much is muddled, contradictory, doubled up, or maybe even unnecessary. As individuals, teams, and organizations begin to think about defining the work before defining the people, they cut through a ton of competition, politics, inefficiency, and unstated and unaligned goals. By definition, the framework of each person being the steward of multiple roles pushes school teams and cultures toward their guiding purpose of helping students succeed and thrive.

Managing roles is working when . . .

There's a greater sense of being alive. People feel that they can leverage their talents and skills against a clear purpose. They are free to step into the authority of their roles and pursue their passion as it aligns with organizational needs.

Teams and organizations have a clear and motivating purpose. Defining purpose and building roles to support that purpose brings clarity and direction to our work. Rather than accepting static job descriptions that can be outdated and ineffective, we expect roles to evolve over time to best serve the purpose. By focusing on the work first, instead of getting caught up in people politics, we can keep the purpose at the center of what we do and have people step in to energize work that moves us forward. When each of us acts as a steward of multiple roles, we are agreeing to make smart decisions about how to prioritize all the work we could be doing in any moment so that we can best move the organization's purpose forward.

Everyone is continuously evolving, improving, and aiming higher. Embracing roles is a learning experience for everyone. Whether you are a superintendent or a first-year teacher, the skill of navigating many roles and being an effective sensor for the organization is an ongoing learning process that will improve the leadership skills of every person. By breaking work into modular pieces of roles, we allow people to embrace a diversity of work and stretch themselves to the benefit of their own development and organizational outcomes.

• •

CHAPTER 4

Decision Making

Aim for "Safe Enough to Try" Instead of Consensus

Chances are, you've already made thousands of decisions today. It might sound absurd, but researchers at Cornell University estimate that you make an average of 221 decisions a day about food alone (Lang, 2006). Over the course of any given day, you will likely make close to 30,000 decisions. You are a decision-making machine. It's a skill you've developed over a lifetime of being faced with choices.

But what happens when a group of expert decision makers (adults) get in a room to make a decision together? Gridlock, lobbying, analysis paralysis, jockeying for power, hurt feelings, cliques, and heated tempers. How is it that as adults who make thousands of decisions a day, we struggle with making decisions that will serve the central missions of our organizations? How do we become so bogged down that we delay the progress we want to make in our classrooms, committees, and districts?

The Problem

Relying on a limited set of tools, many groups settle into a pattern of endless meetings with endless discussion to move decision making forward. Too often, we leave with more questions than we had before and little idea of what decisions were made, what's next, and who is accountable.

> How is it that as adults who make thousands of decisions a day, we struggle with making decisions that will serve the central missions of our organizations?

The monetary cost of these meetings is extraordinary. This issue is so salient that there is actually a Harvard Business School app that will help you estimate the monetary impact of meetings in your particular circumstances ("Estimate the Cost of a Meeting," 2016).

The human cost is even starker.

THE CYCLE OF MEETING PARALYSIS

Every day we walk into meetings hoping to come to agreement and make crucial decisions. In a traditional organization, you prepare for a meeting by sending out pre-reading, but it's likely that most of the people won't have read it. You go through an agenda, trying to provide background and context so everyone can align on some next steps.

Yet in spite of the time devoted to the issue, once the meeting is over there may be side conversations. You may be included in those water cooler discussions, but many times you are not. On the positive side, these conversations may involve people who are trying to get more clarity or who are charged with developing more detailed ideas by soliciting additional feedback and information. On the negative side, some people will use these side conversations to gain support for their questioning of the merits of a decision or the authority of the person making it.

Then another meeting comes around where you are asked to provide an update. More questions come up from the last meeting. Rather than moving toward clear decisions that people can then act on—and learn from—people continue to circle around the issues. After the meeting, you become more confused as you try to incorporate everyone's feedback. So then there are more side meetings and consulting with higher-ups.

For larger projects, especially planning projects, the regular updates get pretty dense, too. As people get busy, they have no ability to provide valuable input, yet the meetings continue to take place and the majority of discussion time is spent recapping, getting people up to speed, and providing clarification. The motivation for the work and the original sense of purpose wane.

This pattern is incredibly common. Though it seems like work is happening, decision making and action taking are repeatedly delayed.

THE RISKS OF DELAYED DECISION MAKING

The decisions we don't make, and the time we waste in not making them, end up delaying necessary support for our students. Delays like this reverberate throughout our organizations and impact all levels. Often the effects are so global and pervasive they are hard to see, but they're real and sometimes glaring. A case in point: One district shared that its teacher recognition program was running two years behind, meaning you would get your five-year gift and letter of recognition on your seventh anniversary. What is the impact of this type of ineffectualness on the culture of an organization? What is the message when a meaningful gesture is reduced to a joke because of inefficiencies and an inability to change?

> *This pattern is incredibly common. Though it seems like work is happening, decision making and action taking are repeatedly delayed.*

Countless times, teachers will say they often learn about a new strategic plan in the third year of a five-year plan. By that time, the relevant technology, resources, and conditions all have changed. The information you used during the planning process may be not only irrelevant but actually wrong. The delay in planning results in substantial risk because the conditions you intended to address at the outset may have changed dramatically. No wonder we continuously blame schools for implementing poorly.

THE FALSE PROMISE OF CONSENSUS . . .
OR DEFAULTING TO A DECIDER-IN-CHIEF

You might say to yourself, "Consensus is hard, and yes, meetings can be tedious, but it's the only way to make sure everyone's voice is heard." If this is you, the word *consensus* can make you feel warm and fuzzy with thoughts of inclusion. On the other hand, the thought of consensus might trigger your fight-or-flight response. In either case, our experience tells us that consensus is an often misused tool and that there are much more effective ways to make decisions. And it's not necessary to default to an autocratic, top-down approach either.

> Countless times, teachers will say they often learn about a new strategic plan in the third year of a five-year plan. By that time, the relevant technology, resources, and conditions all have changed.

One scenario for consensus building is the situation where "the smartest people" are brought together to tackle a significant problem or to develop a strategic plan. Usually there is a kick-off brainstorming session, and everything gets thrown on the wall, including the kitchen sink. You work together to organize common themes, but in the end you still have ten to fifteen topics and you have agreed to focus on three.

In order to whittle it down to three, you go through some sort of polling process, and this is where the consensus building comes into play. The use of voting or polling makes the process feel democratic, but it provides a false sense of alignment. Consensus as a default way of making decisions can lead to unintended consequences, such as these:

1. *Shifting accountability.* When there isn't clear decision-making authority, and decisions are made by a group of people, it's easy for folks to point fingers at others if the result isn't positive. People will go around and around on who said what, why they did or didn't really support it, and whose fault it is instead of focusing on taking ownership for their role and learning from the decision.

2. *Mediocre solutions.* When we focus on averaging all opinions, we overlook options that are unique or above average. If there

are roles with clear expertise and valid data, why does it make sense to water down ideas rather than make the smartest decision to help us fulfill the purpose of our work?

3. *Failure to empathize.* To move decisions forward with consensus, people often get pressured to agree. By pressuring dissenters to conform, rather than giving them the space to work through their resistance, concerns, and data that might be integrated, you risk the disengagement of people in key roles. If *everyone* is a valuable human sensor, then each team member is as vital as every other. It means everyone participating has a purpose and their contribution is needed.

In today's complex educational institutions, with the pushes and pulls of national and local policies, trends in pedagogy, community engagement, and other competing agendas, almost every decision has to be "socialized," "agreed upon," or some way part of a "consensus." It's what seems fair, and it suggests that a particular goal and plan has widespread support.

> *By systematically outvoting dissenters, rather than giving them the space to work through their resistance, concerns, and data that might be integrated, you risk the disengagement of people in key roles.*

Consensus has its origins in religious and cultural contexts, like the early Quaker meeting rules. Historically, consensus building has also been called "alternative dispute resolution." In this context, consensus-building participants seek a mutually acceptable resolution of differences, or it is used as a means to bring a group together around a greater purpose.

When consensus is used to build trust, or to meaningfully involve communities that have traditionally been silenced, it can be a powerful tool. Big decisions that will directly impact each member of a group could be a good candidate for consensus. A decision about the core team of a startup taking a pay cut to onboard a new sales leader is an example.

However, the overuse of consensus as a decision-making tool, or the misuse of consensus as the default for all decisions, is a sign of underlying problems. So what other options do we have? If not consensus, do we default to individual, autocratic decisions?

Top-down decisions *do* manage to avoid the time and human capital investment of consensus, but they have their own downfalls. Depending on the style of communication, it can feel like "my way or the highway" to everyone else, or it can imply that "I have the expertise to know best, and decisions will always be reviewed and second-guessed by me."

We see this type of top-down management in some school districts that have brought in a new superintendent or new school principal to "fix" the problems. There are three key issues we hear over and over again in school districts with this management style. First, top-down management is dependent on a heroic leader, and many superintendents don't stick around long enough for some of their decisions to be implemented or sustained. Second, many decisions are still slow to show up and make an impact in actual classrooms. And third, often the decisions are uninformed by the actual needs of the teachers on the front line.

What we want to do is take the advantages of both these management styles and minimize the effects of the downsides. To help us strategize around this approach we can repurpose a simple 2 x 2 to illustrate the tension between competing priorities. A tension map illustrates the advantages and disadvantages of two strategies that appear mutually exclusive. In this example we will call it group consensus versus top-down decision making. In actuality, the choice between these two options does not have to be an either/or. A tension map can show us the advantages of both and allow us to leverage both in a complementary way. In fact, what the map will show us is that focusing on one priority to the exclusion of the other can lead to serious downsides. Leaders who are adept at managing tensions are often the most successful.

The tension map strategy is simple. Place the two strategies atop a quadrant. Add plus and minus signs to illustrate the advantages and disadvantages of focusing on each, as shown at the top of the opposite page.

Now that you have the basic structure, you can fill it out. For the advantages, ask yourself what the positive results of focusing on that strategy would be. For the disadvantages, list the downsides to over-focusing on this strategy to the exclusion of the other. A filled out version of the tension map strategy is given at the bottom of the opposite page.

Once the map is filled out, you can design a decision-making process to capture the advantages of the different approaches. For

Traditional Models of Decision Making: Tension Map Template

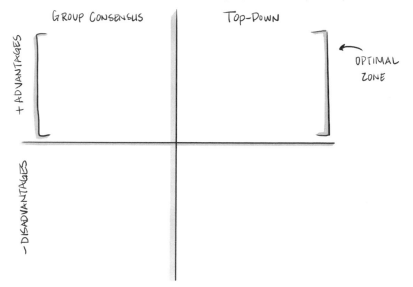

example, a meeting process that gives everyone space to weigh in, but final decisions are made only by people with the authority and experience in that area. For the downside, it can be helpful to highlight early warning signs or indications that you might be focusing too much on one strategy to the exclusion of the other. Use this

Traditional Models of Decision Making: Completed Tension Map

GROUP CONSENSUS | TOP-DOWN

+ ADVANTAGES
- Everyone is engaged
- Get team buy-in
- More complete picture of data and information

- Fast
- Someone with experience makes the final decision
- Clarity about who is making decision

← OPTIMAL ZONE

- DISADVANTAGES
- Slow
- End up with the average of all opinions

- Can feel disempowering to team
- One person may make decisions with limited data

as a map to guide you through opportunity and away from risk. Creating a plan that maximizes the advantages and can steer away from early warning signs takes creativity and initiative. It can feel like trying out a new baseball swing. The elements are all familiar, but they are put together in a new way.

....

The New Rule

Aim for "Safe Enough to Try" Instead of Consensus

We're not stuck with the decision-making delays and quagmires we've come to tolerate and even accept. When staff and school teams work with the New Rule of *aim for "safe enough to try"*—a phrase that is used in the practice of Holacracy (Robertson, 2015)—*instead of consensus*, it can become a mantra that empowers teams to take action. It's a learn-by-doing approach that treats decision making more like a team sport than a spectator pastime.

> *When we learn to make decisions quickly—with the right purpose, people, information, and levels of risk—we create a sense of possibility. And more, we demonstrate that we value our teams, students, and teachers.*

When we learn to make decisions quickly—with the right purpose, people, information, and levels of risk—we create a sense of possibility. And more, we demonstrate that we value our teams, students, and teachers.

The model we propose is a self-advocacy approach to decision making. It's a blended approach that sits all the important roles around the table—literally or figuratively. But instead of seeking either total consensus or a top-down judge, it empowers the person doing the work to make the decision. The emphasis on self-advocacy shifts the dynamic from passive to active, from fuzziness to clarity, from participant to owner. It defaults to "safer" decisions that are smaller in scope or narrower in impact in order to create momentum. The aim of "safe enough to try" is to learn from experience, not fears, and make decisions about specific issues that can be decided on rather than global and even philosophical points that have no concrete solutions.

The self-advocacy model leads to powerful underlying shifts and benefits:

- It requires clarity about exactly who (which role) is accountable for an area of work and decision making, cutting through confusion, competition, land grabbing, overanalyzing, and even hiding.

- It requires that the decision maker think through exactly what data, expertise, resources, or advice they need in order to make the decision.

> *The aim of "safe enough to try" is to learn from experience, not fears, and make decisions about specific issues that can be decided on rather than global and even philosophical points that have no concrete solutions.*

- It requires the owner of the decision to make proposals (recommendations) about solutions in a very specific way so they get exactly the feedback and information that is needed. Having a strict protocol to process these proposals eliminates the potential for noise to confuse the issue and the real feedback that is needed.

- It makes decision making transparent by making it clear who is accountable for the decisions, allowing for individuals to provide additional information and data points.

- It puts emphasis on making decisions and creating solutions that are "safe enough to try" so the owner can keep things moving forward.

- It spreads decision making and ownership, thus building capacity for the benefit of the whole learning community.

- Finally, it assumes decisions will move forward, and it is incumbent on the person who has an issue or concern to demonstrate how that issue or concern would move the organization backward.

The whole self-advocacy approach frames decisions in a new light. Imagine yourself as a role holder who is making a proposal for a decision. Simply starting the discussion with "I propose that . . ." instead of asking "What should we do?" shifts the dynamic of the discussion. Then, as you move the discussion forward, imagine yourself soliciting feedback with a question like "Is this safe enough to try?" By soliciting feedback with "safe enough to try" rather than "Does everyone agree?" gives you the opportunity to

> *Simply starting the discussion with "I propose that . . ." instead of asking "What should we do?" shifts the dynamic of the discussion.*

capture important data and feedback about your proposal to make it better, without the constraint of waiting for total consensus to move forward. You're the advocate and owner of what you need in order to make a decision. You're not expected to get permission or consensus from others in the meeting. Instead, you are making others aware of what is going on so that they can consider how it impacts their own work. They can prevent your work from moving forward only if they can demonstrate that it is unsafe to try for the organization or it creates new issues for their own work that need to be resolved.

Supported with the right information and insight, this self-advocacy approach allows us to make decisions smarter and faster for students and, in doing so, spreading the benefits of "safe enough to try."

Let's take a look at how this rule can be put into action.

. . . .

CASE STUDY

Case Study: Solving a Curriculum Adoption Stalemate

Reggie, an assistant superintendent in a midwestern school district in the suburbs of a major city, was nearly drowning in frustration over how long it was taking for his district to decide on the curriculum it would adopt for the next five years. He had been through the lengthy process before, but with the rapidly expanding variety of digital options that were a desired and necessary part of the mix, the information-gathering process was more arduous than ever and there were loud and competing opinions.

The team set up to make this decision included nine people from the district's senior cabinet. The team comprised the superintendent; the assistant superintendent preK–6; the assistant superintendent 7–adult;

the heads of educator effectiveness, school improvement, and human resources; the chief of finance; and a couple of others.

With these district leaders in the room, each responsible for a department, we believe they were unknowingly stalling the process. Each had their opinion of what they needed. Trying to integrate all the inputs across departments and grade levels seemed to result in requirements for something very customized and complex. They were aiming to get consensus around a very big chunk of work, which included a curriculum adoption across grade levels, spanning multiple departments, and encompassing multiple subject areas.

To reset the team and regain momentum, the assistant superintendent of educator effectiveness decided to get everyone in a room together for a whole day without intrusions. The idea would be to identify a path that would allow them to move forward with a curriculum decision. They would need to agree on how they would make the decision and who needed to be part of that process.

The first step was to revisit and crystalize the purpose of the curriculum, which had become muddled amid all the competing points of view. Then they needed to get more concrete about the specific decisions that had to be made in order to finalize a curriculum adoption. They also realized there were too many cooks in the kitchen. Everyone needed to be there to provide input, but they had to figure out how to integrate everyone's seemingly divergent opinions.

The reset meeting was structured with the following agenda to allow the team to refine their purpose, agree on a process to make this decision going forward, and let everyone be heard:

Hour 1: Checking In. The first hour was spent checking in, getting everyone focused on the work ahead, and primarily revisiting and refining the purpose of the team. The purpose changed from

The team making a decision about curriculum

to

The team informing the person who needed to make the decisions for each grade level's curriculum

In reality, the success of this part of the meeting could be attributed to the acknowledgment that there were different expectations and confusion over the purpose of the team as well as disagreement over who was doing what. It's important to note that like in any meeting there were some people who liked to talk more than their fair share and others who didn't contribute at all. Fortunately, there was a meeting facilitator to ensure that everyone engaged in the meeting equally.

Hours 2–3: Breaking Down Curriculum. Once the group had begun opening up about the challenges and expectations, it was time to dig in and get more concrete. The work began by developing a common understanding of curriculum. This sounds so basic, but with fast-changing roles, teaching methods, and technology, familiar concepts can mean lots of different things to different people. Does curriculum include teaching tools, standards maps, assessments, and so on? Should we think about curriculum differently for elementary, middle, and high schools?

In this portion of the meeting, one person proposed to the group that they should organize their thinking about curriculum into three categories: guided leveled content, adaptive content, and customized content. This made sense and no one had any objections to this approach, so they immediately began applying this filter to their decision making.

Guided leveled content was applied to learning maps and pacing guides for teachers. *Adaptive content* included all the digital and online content they were deciding on for their blended learning initiative. *Customized content* included all the individual lessons that teachers were creating to meet the needs of their students but weren't shared across their district or across other districts. For example, one teacher was creating rap videos to engage students in math lessons.

Once these categories were defined, the group needed to understand how each category addressed particular aspects of learning, including the workload of the teacher, the personalized experience for the student, and different levels of learning and depth of knowledge. Ideally, each of the three curriculum elements would support one or more aspects of learning.

As the group moved through this process, we could see lights go on in people's eyes as they started to realize how much simpler it was to discuss each element when it was broken down into smaller components. Some of the tension and confusion seemed to be released from their shoulders. They were becoming eager to get to the next step of the process, which only increased their energy and enthusiasm.

Hours 4–5: The Three-Plate Exercise. This part of the meeting was focused on defining which components of the curriculum were needed by grade level to see if there were different needs in the elementary, middle, and high schools.

For this activity, a sheet of paper with pictures of three plates was passed out to each administrator. Each plate was labeled Elementary, Middle, or High. Here were the directions:

> *You have three ingredients—guided leveled content, adaptive content, and customized content. Please create your ideal mix of curriculum in each plate by grade level.*

Even though each person worked independently, the team was surprised by how similar their plates looked. For example, the team thought that elementary schools needed about 60 percent guided leveled content, 30 percent adaptive content, and 10 percent teacher-created customized activities. For high schools, also working independently, they concluded that approximately 30 percent needed to be guided leveled content, 30 percent needed to be digital adaptive, and 40 percent needed to be teacher-created customized activities. As they completed this process, the team realized that while they were having a lot of general discussion around curriculum, each person and suggestion was coming from a different context and to solve different needs, which had been driving their conversations in circles.

Equally interesting, the team collectively recognized that each person on the team offered insight from their unique context and background information. In fact, each person was a valuable data point for the eventual decision maker to consider. One person thought that since high school teachers are content experts they would want to deliver their own content. Another person thought that since students in their district come into high school at all different levels, too much grade-level structured content wouldn't be helpful.

Hour 6: Deciding on Decision Makers. The team was left with the question they started with: How was a final decision going to get made about the curriculum? That's what the final hour focused on.

After the productive work of the day, it became more evident that the assistant superintendent of preK–6 was accountable for academic results for the early grades and therefore should make the decision on curriculum, incorporating data from the others but not relying on consensus or trying to integrate and negotiate the decisions with everyone else.

Once this decision and process were agreed to, a cascade of other decisions followed. The assistant superintendent of 7–adult was given the decision-making role for the curriculum for the secondary grades. The assistant superintendent of educator effectiveness took on the role of training their school leaders and teachers on a similar process. Each school had to reflect on how it would utilize curriculum.

After the workshop, one of the assistant superintendents said, "This is so incredibly simple. Why didn't we think of it?" Too many of us have it stuck in our minds that we need all the right people around the table to make a decision. Usually this approach leads to consensus building, which is a long drawn-out negotiation. At the same time, something that seems as simple as curriculum adoption isn't simple at all because it's a combination of a lot of smaller decisions. Simplicity is hard to define, but perhaps to get to simple you have to get to "not difficult" or maybe "safe enough to try."

Lessons

Our school districts are filled with people who are smart and really care about the work, yet we continue to run into failure on one initiative after another. It doesn't have to be that way. Change may feel uncomfortable and difficult, but the reality is we are trying to break decision-making and meeting habits that have been developed over a long period of time. Here are the cornerstone lessons for the self-advocacy approach to decision making:

- Get aligned and clear out the noise.

- Decide on things you *can* decide on: make decisions smaller.

- Fail forward: approach planning and big decisions as decision cycles.

GET ALIGNED AND CLEAR OUT THE NOISE

Decision making isn't possible until the decision to be made is clear. Too many side issues, too many caveats and eventualities—in other words, too much noise—can defeat efforts for responsive decisions that are timely and useful. Which leads to this point: Having a lot of people on a team doesn't mean you're getting the input the team needs.

> Having a lot of people on a team doesn't mean you're getting the input the team needs.

Competing opinions, needs, and new ideas will always be in the air, creating a mix of excitement, stress—and noise. But decisions can't be made without clarity on exactly what needs to be decided on. It's essential for teams and stewards for specific work and decisions to get aligned on the following:

- the goals for the decision to be made (purpose)

- what the issues are and who is affected by a decision (sensors and data needed)

- who has the needed expertise, experience, and information (the role of steward for the decision)

For example, Anthony remembers one school telling him that it had tried multiple online math programs for the ninth graders and none of them seemed to work. Its ninth graders were consistently coming in at third- to sixth-grade levels. Out of frustration and under pressure from various constituents, the cycle of searching for new programs to solve the problem became the norm. But improvements weren't coming and more ideas, pressure, and noise were thrown into the mix.

The facts showed that the school's current math products were set to reading levels that were too high. The students never had a chance because most of the time they struggled to comprehend the directions. Often they were guessing to understand what the math problem was and what they needed to do. This is a small example of something that happens every day in schools across the country. In this case, the school either needed a math program that could adapt to different reading levels or needed to get these kids to grade-level reading.

In the example above, the purpose was to find a better math program that would result in students getting better math scores, but it was missing the mark. Perhaps the team's purpose should have been focused on understanding why students were struggling year over year, regardless of the math program. So often when we are presented with a project or a problem and hastily form teams, we are distracted by all the voices giving their opinions and solutions, and we spend very little time understanding the true purpose of the team and how to move forward with the work.

Once the team is clear on the purpose, the role authority for the decisions that need to be made can be clarified. This immediately eliminates a lot of noise. It puts the focus on what the work is that needs to get done. You don't have to anticipate your future needs; just focus on what you know for a fact now. You can always add roles to a team as the needs of the work change. It is essential to concentrate on the work to be done and focus only on what you know now versus anticipating work. Otherwise, you can spend endless hours anticipating what may happen without concrete data. All those related and potential issues add to the noise, confusion, and competing ideas, distracting from actual decision making. We habitually try to anticipate and predict the future in our work on projects. The bigger the decision, the farther out in the future we want to predict. The farther our predictions stretch out, the less accurate they become.

We've all been in big meetings with a lot of people because we are anticipating all of the current and future stakeholders. When decisions and contributors on teams get this big, decisions, feedback, and plans are being made on unclear or antici-

> *The bigger the decision, the farther out in the future we want to predict. The farther our predictions stretch out, the less accurate they become.*

pated information. The reason we often end up second-guessing ourselves on these types of big decisions is that everyone has a different point of view on what happens in the future.

When teams can focus on the purpose of the work and identify what is noise and what are data, they lay the foundation for decisions that are manageable and that feel safe enough to try.

DECIDE ON THINGS YOU *CAN* DECIDE ON: MAKE DECISIONS SMALLER

Getting clear often requires that you get more specific, not only about people but about the problem. You can think of this as a lesson to decide on things that *can be* decided on.

You might need to "peel back the layers" of a decision or initiative in order to identify smaller components that can be defined and addressed. You might need to limit the scope, time frame, or affected community. You might need to envision the decision as an experiment that is "safe enough to try" but also safe enough *and successful enough* to continue.

As we saw with the case study of a school district struggling to make a curriculum adoption decision, breaking down decisions into manageable chunks speeds up the

> *Breaking down decisions into manageable chunks speeds up the process enormously.*

process enormously. It will feel counterintuitive that making ten smaller decisions is quicker than one big one, but as you read in the case study, that first small decision could help all the other decisions fall into place.

As an analogy, think of the planning that goes into building a cathedral versus planning a farmers market. When you plan for a cathedral, you take years or a decade to design every little piece. It can take decades to centuries to complete the construction.

You can imagine that by the time the cathedral is finished, all the assumptions, the project team, and the needs of the community may have changed. If, for example, the population doubled since the plan was completed decades before, you may already need an addition.

As a rule, cathedrals were built as massive structures that would be a beacon and could accommodate centuries of evolving needs, but way too often these projects were misses. One of the most famous examples of this is Gaudi's Barcelona cathedral La Sagrada Familia. Construction started in 1882, and the builders predicted that it would take thirteen years to complete. In 2013, it was only 65 percent complete and is now expected to be finished in 2026.

A farmers market is the cathedral's natural opposite. It is can be put up quickly. Tents of different sizes with different offerings are erected each week. Some may stay or go. Farmers markets still require planning, but they are dynamic. The farmers market makes adjustments based on new information coming in week over week.

Farmers markets work on weekly decision cycles. After each Sunday, they look at the data to make decisions about how big to make certain tents, what sold more, where the foot traffic was bottlenecking, and so on. By next Sunday they should have a better market because they are constantly adjusting and tweaking as they get new information and conditions change.

School districts often feel like they have to stick with a decision and let it play out, even if they sense it needs to be reevaluated. The thought of reconvening everyone to go through the process of evaluation and change is daunting. It already took a long time to get to the current decision. To do it again would delay the project even more. This is where smaller decisions come into play again. With smaller decisions, you can move forward with the concept of "safe enough to try." These smaller decisions and actions provide new data that inform the next set of decisions that need to be made. By operating on decision cycles, your organization is embracing a continuous improvement model.

School districts and organizations often say they are about continuous improvement but are not clear about how often or how they do it. Is your organization on decision-making and improvement cycles that are one to two weeks long or one year long? With annual data and reflection, how long would it take to analyze and implement changes for the next cycle?

FAIL FORWARD: APPROACH PLANNING AND BIG DECISIONS AS DECISION CYCLES

At IDEO, the boundary-pushing design firm, this idea of *iterating forward* is a core strategy used with clients. It sounds simple, but it presupposes a specific mindset, one that is able to let go of ideas and build them before they might feel truly ready or fully baked. This kind of mindset accepts that failure is a natural outcome of efforts. In fact, failure can sometimes provide some of the richest data to help shape efforts going forward.

Alexis learned this lesson when she was an undergraduate biology student working in a lab at her university:

> *I remember my experiment had failed to produce the hypothesized results and I was deflated. My professor told me this should be celebrated. In a world of incalculable possibility, you know one thing is definitely NOT the right answer. And to uncover that with certainty, is a good thing. This simple sentiment changed the way I looked at failure forever. Now I know this simple truth. It is normal to fail; it is unacceptable not to learn from it.*

In education, the stakes are so high that we do everything to avoid failure. But let's look at it like this. Failure is already happening, no? All learning means practice, errors, failure, and success, with steps forward and backward in a positive direction. Despite your painstaking efforts to plan the failure out of every initiative, there are challenges and shortsightedness and all kinds of issues that are popping up.

Look at a project like inBloom, the nonprofit established by the Bill & Melinda Gates Foundation. It was a $100 million initiative to standardize data that was shuttered in 2014. After that huge failure, the Gates Foundation and its partners wrote it off by saying they "learned a lot from it." The learning for this massive and expensive project was summarized in a couple bullet points. Interestingly, in 2015 a federally funded Carnegie Mellon University project, LearnSphere, rebooted the ideas to push it forward as an educational research project. InBloom had decided to make its software open source, but it's not clear how LearnSphere will proceed at this point.

What's worse than this hundred million dollar "lesson"? It's the fact that we continue to make similar mistakes because so many of our plans are so large and complex. Think back to the cathedral analogy. Why not attempt smaller, more iterative changes and then use failure to refine and hone ideas so that they get stronger over time?

> *Why not attempt smaller, more iterative changes and then use failure to refine and hone ideas so that they get stronger over time?*

This is different than the concept of a pilot, which usually means testing or trying a complete program before introducing it more widely within controlled conditions or a perfect scenario. "Safe enough to try" implies an experimental, minimal viable product approach where not all of the actions are clear. The goal is to determine whether the assumptions are right and then build on that learning to make new assumptions and test those. It might feel more like a gradual release of features or complexity based on learnings at each milestone.

In a school district we worked with, one of the middle schools has been a historically low-performing school. In the 2015–2016 school year, the principal decided to try blended learning. Instead of focusing on pullout intervention programs and increasing assessments, he made an unpopular decision to push teachers toward personalizing learning for each student and to think about the classroom model in new ways.

The school board and many of the traditionalists in the school district were skeptical, but when the school board made their first visit to the school, they were blown way. Although specific state data about the academic results were not out yet, the teachers and students were clearly more engaged and happier than they had ever been before. The culture of the school had completely changed. Academic results in schools are sustained by student engagement and school culture, not programs and initiatives. In this case it might be tempting to say, well, it's easy to select the worst-performing school and give it a try. Sure, that's true. However, the difference in this case was the principal had a choice in proposing a solution to the school's performance problems. While others objected to the approach, they couldn't block his decision; the principle had the clear authority.

When you work on a decision-making cycle or cadence, as described in Chapter 1, you are constantly updating your plan based on new information. Each small decision provides new information to make the next decision. For example, in the case study, we talked about the assistant superintendent of preK–6 making some decisions about the primary school curriculum adoption. At the same time, the assistant superintendent of educator effectiveness decided to train the school leaders on how to think about the curriculum they used and be more purposeful with their choices. These decisions were made with new information determined from the workshop. A more typical next step for a school district might have been to order the curriculum.

As we make more decisions, although they're smaller, it's likely that we will make a few mistakes along the way. When we plan big, we run into denial. We don't want to think about the decisions being made being wrong. We have to proceed forward. We put all our focus on how well we are executing the plan versus thinking about whether the plan is still right.

When we embrace "failing forward," failures and falls are small so we can get up quickly. It's a lot easier to fix a small tent in a farmers market than trying to fix a wing in a cathedral as it's being built. The path to failing forward is through the self-advocacy model of decision making. It allows people to make decisions that are manageable and in their control.

• •

Experimenting With Decision Making

Remember: Experiments are designed as trials to be tested out, iterated, studied, and broadly implemented over time. Try out and adapt the experiments on decision making to fit your role and context.

The decisions we don't make, and the time we waste in not making them, end up delaying necessary support for students. "Safe enough to try" is a maxim that can guide you out of decision-making conundrums, endless consensus seeking, or the analysis paralysis that we so frequently run into when we try to make decisions together. If you're excited about the prospect of more autonomy, self-advocacy, nimbleness, and continuously responding to the new information coming your way, here are some tools and how-tos to get you started.

EXPERIMENT 8

Three Language Shifts for Decision-Making Discussions

In the book *Holacracy,* Brian J. Robertson (2015) acknowledges that not everyone has the authority to make major and even radical changes to the structure of their organization. To address this, he suggests that language shifts can be a powerful first step toward a broader change. It's something anyone can start regardless of title or tenure in an organization. He writes, "Language is commonly seen as the verbal expression of culture but language can also create culture" (p. 297).

Here are three simple shifts we've seen schools embrace and spread:

1. *Safe enough to try.* As we have discussed throughout the chapter, the New Rule of *aim for "safe enough to try" instead of consensus* is a principle that helps everyone in an organization recalibrate how decisions are made. When used as a frequent, go-to expression, we've seen this simple sentence transform the way teams work together. It will help your team embrace a learn-as-you-go approach and support people in taking risks and innovating. Here's an example:

    COLLEAGUE: "I was thinking about working remotely from each of the schools in my district one day a week to increase my visibility and be a better partner to my principals. Does that plan make sense to you?"

    YOU: "It seems safe enough to try. Go for it."

    Simple, straightforward, done.

2. *Proposals rather than solutions.* "I have a proposal" suggests a recommendation put forward for the consideration of other relevant roles. It implies the possibility for input and iteration. "I have a solution" suggests you've solved the problem. That presumption can freak people out and trigger organizational antibodies to attack. Similar to the recommendations in Experiment 3: Offer Feedback as Data in Chapter 2, this shift in language accomplishes two things. First, it lowers the barrier to entry, allowing people to share proposals rather than waiting for them to be perfect. Second, it encourages people to take ownership of their role and issues. The next time someone

comes to you or a group with a complaint, problem, or frustration, you can ask, "Do you have a proposal or starting idea to address that?" Robertson (2015) explains that using a proposal is "a way to start the conversation from a proactive, creative place, rather than a negative one" (p. 299).

3. *Disagree and commit.* In his 2016 Letter to Shareholders, Jeff Bezos, founder and CEO of Amazon, shared this decision-making mantra that he uses to get decision making out of a rut. When you are in a situation where you want to move something forward but you know you aren't going to reach total consensus, you can recognize dissenters' opinions and at the same time ask them to commit, for speed's sake, with the knowledge that the team can return to this decision and pivot after the impact is well understood. Bezos (2017) went on to talk about this being a responsibility of the manager as well: "This isn't one way. If you're the boss, you should do this too. I disagree and commit all the time. . . . [I]t's not me thinking to myself, 'Well, these guys are wrong and missing the point, but this isn't worth me chasing.' It's a genuine disagreement of opinion, a candid expression of my view, a chance for the team to weigh my view, and a quick, sincere commitment to go their way" (Bezos, 2017, "High-Velocity Decision Making," para. 5).

This act of embracing the unknown and not being afraid to try is a behavior that we can choose to model for our students and ourselves.

EXPERIMENT 9
Protocol for a Starting Proposal

Better decision making as a team requires a balanced approach. Coming into a meeting already committed to a "solution" is bound to raise some eyebrows and defenses, and it can open up the discussion to more backlash than necessary. On the opposite end, coming in with nothing but an open-ended question like "How can we address this issue?" sets up the team for a discussion that can easily get off track.

Enter the proposal. A well-crafted proposal strikes a strategic balance—a concrete starting place for the discussion but still open enough to integrate different perspectives.

If you have an idea, even if it isn't perfect, consider throwing it out at the start of a meeting as a starting proposal. People often worry that coming in with a proposal will make them appear bossy or not inclusive of other ideas. This is where framing becomes important. You could say something like, "Since we are here to discuss how to address this issue, one possible proposal to move us forward is X."

It sounds easy, but proposing an idea can be stressful and may make you feel on the spot. Follow the format below to prepare a starting proposal before a meeting and see how it transforms the discussion.

1. **State the facts.** This is where you set the stage with unfiltered and judgment-free evidence. Focus on the facts, the conditions and happenings that provide context for the pitch to come.
   - What happened that triggered this tension or situation?

2. **State your interpretation.** Take ownership of your story and be transparent.
   - How did you interpret this situation?
   - How did it make you feel?

3. **Summarize and state the importance.** Describe quickly why this tension is important to resolve.
   - Why is this important to the purpose of your team/organization?
   - What do you think the impact of resolving this tension will be?

4. **State the starting proposal.** It doesn't have to be perfect, just a starting point to take one step forward to resolve your tension.
   - Do you need an action or project from another role?
   - Do you want something to *start* happening?
   - Do you want something to *stop* happening?

5. **Call for feedback.** Invite others to share their reactions and data/information that could be helpful.
   - What help do you need from other team members to make this the best proposal possible?
   - Are there experts in the circle who could surface/provide data useful to this proposal?

Here's an example:

- *State the facts:* Last year we hired several consultants to help us design the approach to our school turnaround efforts. The consultants had limited experience working with schools in the past, and the results have been mediocre at best.

- *State your interpretation:* I feel like I've seen this dynamic play out before, bringing in outsiders to try to create a perfect solution rather than investing in experimenting with and building on the ideas we already have.

- *Summarize and state the importance:* It frustrates me, and I think if we can approach it in a different way we can achieve our school turnaround goals.

- *State the starting proposal:* My starting proposal is to form a cross-functional team of teachers and administrators who agree to spend 10 percent of their time implementing and testing turnaround approaches in their schools for the next year.

- *Call for feedback:* I need feedback from the roles on this team to better understand if there is an appetite for this and some ideas that we could implement on a small scale.

There may be many more steps before this proposal is formally adopted, but the powerful clarity of this starting proposal provides a strong start. This approach should be used by every role on a team; even leadership roles can benefit from the proposal process. It balances the two competing poles that we presented in the tension map earlier in the chapter. On the one hand, a decision requires someone to take individual ownership over the issue; on the other hand, good data should be uncovered before a decision is made. By embracing these two truths, you can move decision making forward faster with less risk and more engagement, serving everyone in the learning community.

EXPERIMENT 10

Default to Yes and Defend No— One Decision at a Time

In keeping with the New Rule of *aim for "safe enough to try" instead of consensus*, the decision-making tables are turned to favor action rather than deliberation. The default action is "yes"—you can move forward if the ideas are safe enough to try. The objectors, skeptics, or naysayers need to defend their "no" or questions with data. Ideas can come in imperfect, even half-baked, and are still presumed safe until proved otherwise.

Instead of asking generic, open-ended questions like "What does everyone think?" ask, "Does anyone have data that indicate this proposal is unsafe to try?" For small decisions with a limited scope, think about using the simple language changes that we outlined in Experiment 8. For larger decisions that need more deliberation, the protocol of defaulting to yes and defending no can help you separate concerns that are valid enough to deal with in this moment or are just add-ons or considerations that can be returned to later, once you have more data.

Use this practice with your team—one decision and one proposal at a time:

After presenting a proposal, go around the entire team, and allow each teammate to answer the question: "Does anyone have data that indicate this proposal is unsafe to try?"

At this point people may offer a "Maybe this will happen . . ." or "Have you thought of this yet?" To move the discussion forward, you need to parse through which of these concerns are valid enough to deal with in this moment and which are just add-ons or considerations that can be returned to later once you have more data. To separate the urgent and valid concerns from the invalid ones, probe further by asking for the specific data or information that they have in mind or asking them to describe exactly why they consider it unsafe. After allowing each person to answer this question, you can move forward with your proposal or stop and resolve any valid issues.

From a timing and momentum perspective, this is much more efficient and effective than open-ended discussion. It is rare that in a one-hour meeting you will be able to secure 100 percent consensus, but you might be able to obtain simple consent based on the notion that there are no presently known data that your proposal would be unsafe to try.

Instead of a goal of trying to make everyone happy, the approach of defaulting to yes and defending no allows a team to take one step forward, knowing the decision can be revisited and the direction shifted if indicated by future data.

Here's an example. Let's say you propose a new initiative where upper elementary school students will lead parent-teacher meetings this year. Your proposal includes the following plan: Students will prepare a reflection sheet covering their strengths, areas of improvement, a plan to address them, and the adult help they will need. Teachers will serve as guides for the meetings, offering questions and direction to stay on track. Parents can ask questions of the student and teacher to clarify what's being discussed, and they can take the reflection sheet home for further conversation. At the end of the fifteen-minute meeting, the student is dismissed and the teacher and parent spend ten minutes on any other points that need to be discussed.

Here are some of the concerns you might face:

"If you are going to address parent-teacher meetings, we also need to talk about the scheduling of the meetings."

"What if the students aren't prepared to lead these important discussions, and we end up wasting time?"

Here is where you can clarify:

"Do you have data that indicate this proposal is unsafe to try?"

If the answer is no, then redirect those people to work through those new topics after you've finalized this decision. Staying laser focused on moving forward with one proposal at a time can avoid the well-intentioned decision-making standoffs we often create when everyone has something they want to add to make an idea better or more comprehensive. Also focusing on known data, and not just anticipations or theories, is important because often we let ideas die because of what we anticipate. There are things we'd never know if we didn't try them first.

In this example, if some of the students are unprepared for the discussions, will the harm be so severe that we won't be able to recover our relationships with parents? Or will we be able to salvage some meaning from the meeting and use it as a lesson for the next parent-teacher meeting? Sometimes we should embrace the chance of failure as an opportunity to learn and improve with real concrete data. For the concerns with data that indicate it's unsafe to try, you can work to integrate that feedback into an updated proposal.

Decision Making Is Working When . . .

When an organization is using a self-advocacy model of decision making, the people in the organization feel more open and responsive to the changing conditions around them. Each member of a team feels heard. Collectively, they are moving in the same direction; individually, they are engaged and have a sense of personal authority. You will know your decision-making approach is working when you sense that people are making decisions quickly, without seeking approval. They don't feel roadblocked by others who aren't doing the work. Decision making is working when . . .

There's a greater sense of being alive. Organizations feel alive when every part of the organization is actively sensing, receiving information, and solving problems.

Teams and organizations have a clear and motivating purpose. When a team has a clear purpose and it's the right purpose, then it is inspiring and achievable. When teams see that they are making decisions that get them closer to the goal and a shared—and understood—purpose, they are motivated to do more, go faster, to engage in the work.

Everyone is continuously evolving, improving, and aiming higher. As you make smaller decisions regularly, you will build confidence in your ability to make smart decisions. This practice will increase your fluency and decision-making muscles. As you create a list of accomplishments, new projects and big decisions will not seem as daunting. These successes will allow you to push yourself and your organization to new levels of achievement through heightened awareness of new information, increased responsiveness to making decisions, and confidence that you are doing the right things.

CHAPTER 5

Sharing Information

Harness the Flow and Let Information Go

Do you believe in giving people the information they need to do their best work?

Do you expect teams to share information to enhance problem solving and decision making?

Do you feel you personally go above and beyond in terms of sharing information—except it rarely feels like it's enough?

If you and your people are struggling with the crucial but amorphous work of sharing information, you're not alone. The ideals of open communication, transparency, and honesty are increasingly aspired to. However, there is often a huge gulf between this ideal and reality.

In today's era of unlimited access to information and limitless opportunities to share it, most people lack the understanding and skills to successfully manage what seems like a barrage of noise in our overloaded worlds. We may aim to keep everyone in the loop, but when a memo about an important meeting gets sent out late, it can create blowback for being inconsiderate, not appreciation for being included. When we share a decision and ask for feedback, are we really interested in using that feedback to shape our work, or are we delivering a result that's not open to debate or change?

We can't forget that information has become a form of currency and, at its core, is power. The desire for power can lead us to horde information rather than share it. And even the most well-intentioned information sharer will discover there are critics who say it's too much and others who says it's too little.

What can we make of this messy communication landscape?

The Problem

While most of us have gotten the message that we need to share information in order to have more open, agile, and responsive teams and schools, we're getting tripped up by actions that have the right intent but the wrong results.

> If we haven't built up trust, or when trust breaks down, information sharing can become the most fraught part of our work lives.

We're spending lots of time sharing information—often adding to our workloads and creating more stress rather than less. However, our efforts can drown out the underlying purpose: providing context, exchanging insights and thinking, listening and sensing, and communicating decisions, successes, and challenges. If we haven't built up trust, or when trust breaks down, information sharing can become the most fraught part of our work lives. We can worry about what we're saying, how we're saying it, and what's going to happen once the information gets out—whether in our teams, with our bosses, or in the context of the larger community.

THE NEW SCHOOL RULES

A FALSE SENSE OF TRANSPARENCY

Transparency connotes openness, communication, and accountability. It's a way of operating that allows others to see what decisions and actions are being taken and what issues are being addressed, and it provides a window into the purpose, plans, and priorities of our schools and districts.

Transparency requires the sharing of information, but information sharing alone doesn't mean transparency has been achieved. So much of the data we share need careful curation, context, and a clear purpose to be effective in creating the openness we desire. But a lack of transparency can be the unintentional effect of ineffective information sharing.

> Transparency requires the sharing of information, but information sharing alone doesn't mean transparency has been achieved.

Check-the-Box Transparency. If information is posted to a server, sent out in a mass distribution, or buried in a vaguely titled report, then you may be able to "check the box" and defend yourself for having shared the information. The information is there, isn't it? Yet the information will miss the mark because the way it's been shared is not useful, understood, or even accessible to those who want and need it.

A typical example might be board meeting minutes. The board usually publishes minutes and makes them openly available. However, even assuming you know to locate the right set of minutes, it's usually impossible to understand how decisions in board meetings were made. A dry statement with all the discussion left out will leave the reader feeling unsatisfied with the level of information transparency, while the provider of the information feels like they've met their obligation to be transparent.

Governments try to say they are transparent through vehicles like the Freedom of Information Act. However, you have to be an informed citizen and go through the process of requesting the information, and it's often in raw form. Check-the-box transparency is barely an improvement over secrecy and limited access to information.

One-and-Done Transparency. Making too much information available at once, and only once, is like posting raw data and saying that you are being transparent. By making immense amounts of unsynthesized information available, your intent might be to demonstrate your expertise, position yourself or your point of view on the project as the right one, or perhaps hide information in the pile, especially if you're unclear about the goals or your role. If you don't have a commitment to break through the noise, the essential information that needs to be understood, acted on, or made available for future use won't be heard. Sharing information takes a commitment to communicate.

Selective Transparency. Transparency some of the time, but in an inconsistent fashion, is confusing and can break trust as much as a lack of transparency. It's human nature to want to crow about good news, bury negative news, and avoid anything that makes us look inept. When we have bad news, the message is often wordsmithed, formalized, and even filtered. When we don't treat the sharing of good news and bad news equally, it can limit our ability to learn from failure and it creates suspicion about what is not being said.

Within a leadership team, selective transparency can show up when different people have different criteria for when information is ready to be shared. One person might feel it's okay to share information as soon as they know it, without coordinating with other leaders on the team, while another member might feel there has to be a unified message first. The challenge with forming a unified message across a team is that it takes time; it often dilutes some of the raw aspects of the information and feels less authentic.

INFORMATION HAS AN EXPIRATION DATE

One other type of false transparency is what we can think of as delayed transparency. The need for speed in sharing information has increased rapidly in recent years. We no longer think in terms of days and weeks—much less semesters. We think in terms of instant and hourly updates and responses.

> *We need to get our information out to people much sooner than we might think— otherwise it sours like milk.*

This means information has an expiration date. Information you hear in the morning may evolve and change by the afternoon. We can't operate in real-time, but in an environment that does, we need a major shift in our thinking. We need to get our information out to people much sooner than we might think—otherwise it sours like milk.

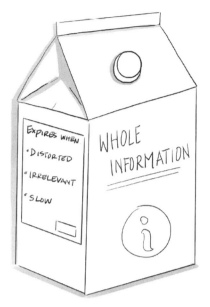

There are two ways information expires today:

1. *Distortion of meaning.* One way information expires is that an originally good message sours because the message was too complicated and slow to pass on. As a result, each time it was passed on it got more and more spoiled—more and more distorted. Remember the game Telephone? The first person in a circle whispers a phrase to the next person, and so on, until the last person says the phrase out loud and everyone hears how it changed from the original.

   A message that is fuzzy, contradictory, or complex is hard to pass on. Without initial clarity, there's not a foundation to build on for greater depth and nuance. And without some repetition, a message doesn't sink in—it doesn't become memorable, and it sours.

2. *Relevance degradation.* The other way information expires is when it isn't useful or consumable for the audience it's going to. Think of your e-mail inbox. Haven't you flagged e-mails you thought were important but were too dense to read immediately? Weeks later, you review outstanding messages and decide you don't need to read most of them anyway. Maybe assumptions or priorities for the project have changed. Essentially, the relevance of those e-mails expired.

Information can expire—go sour—not only when is sits around in an inbox or pile, or awaits approval. The information can arrive in a timely fashion, but the recipient may be overwhelmed or too busy

> *Placing the burden on the recipient to find, manage, assess, and engage with all the information leads to conflict and disengagement when people feel ignored, on the one hand, or overburdened, on the other.*

to deal with it, be unclear about what's being asked, or basically be in a state of MEGO, or "my eyes glaze over." Without useful context and an engaging approach, the information will never be consumed, much less responded to.

Placing the burden on the recipient to find, manage, assess, and engage with all the information leads to conflict and disengagement when people feel ignored, on the one hand, or overburdened, on the other.

 New Rule

Harness the Flow and Let Information Go

Many of us know the parable of "The Blind Men and the Elephant," where one blind man feels a tail and says the object is scratchy and another blind man feels the trunk and says the object has a curvy shape and goes up and down like a seesaw. And the third blind man feels a tusk and says for certain the object is hard and pointy. The story is used to teach us that limited access and overreaching misinterpretation will lead to misinformation.

One person with limited touch and reach can have only a limited version of reality. Although each blind man's description is right, they are all wrong. In a connected world, we've learned that we can collaborate and share to make better decisions and have more accurate insights.

As teams work together and as we communicate our findings and plans to others, we learn and inform each other to understand the bigger picture. The same process holds true for all the interested constituencies. Parents, the wider public, agencies, and other stakeholders can understand and support the mission of our schools and initiatives if they understand the whole picture and not just the one part.

Yet this kind of communication takes forethought and practice. In a world where we are constantly connected, are pulled in many directions for attention, and have a multitude of sources of information, we've gotten used to messages that are designed for Twitter and Facebook; many of us prefer the briefest of text messages and e-mails. Maybe with an emoji thrown in. Yet we clearly need more information than that to make important decisions. And we need that information in ways that make sense to us.

We can think of ourselves in terms of the dual roles of being information providers and information receivers. The responsibility of information providers is to figure out how best to engage receivers with the information they are sharing. The responsibility of information receivers is to pay attention to information according to its purpose, look for information that may be readily available, and ask for more information or clarification if the information isn't accessible, useful, or needed; they need to actively process the information and provide feedback to the information provider to influence their work.

Sharing information is a form of exchange. Without information "landing," it hasn't really been shared. If people aren't getting it, we have a responsibility to try again with a new approach, or we may need to admit that our "great idea" actually wasn't so great or wasn't meeting the real needs of receivers.

When as receivers we aren't getting it or are feeling left out, we need to consider what we're missing. Is it

> Sharing information is a form of exchange. Without information "landing," it hasn't really been shared.

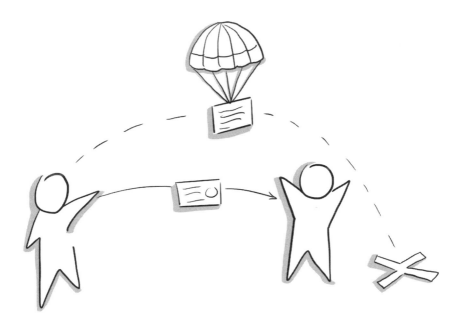

information we need to accomplish our immediate work or information we hope will make us feel included—and what will help meet that need? If you aren't getting information, it's your responsibility to speak up and advocate for the information—and the understanding—you need.

Thus the new rule for sharing information, *harness the flow and let information go*, is based on the premise that communication is relational, not transactional. It's the opposite of false and delayed transparency. You're thinking about how information can be shared in ways that are accessible, open, timely, and probably imperfect. All these qualities build trust and make information more useful.

With a model of relational not transactional transparency, the following happens:

- People can access or ask for the information they need to fulfill their purpose.

- They have shared practices around who, what, when, where, and how to share information, which builds trust and saves time—people know what's expected.

- Team members want to share information with others.

- Habits and routines for sharing information with the public are communicated and regularly improved upon.

- Information is shared in ways that show respect and recognition for the audience of the information.

Trust is such an important currency in today's education organization. When information is shared in a relational and not transactional way, it plays a critical role in building trust.

> *Communication is relational, not transactional.*

....

CASE STUDY

Case Study: Saying It Fast, Often, and Creatively

In Arizona, near the Mexican border about three hours' drive from Phoenix with not much in between, is a town whose school district has 8,000 students across seventeen schools. The community has the state's highest unemployment rate at 19 percent. The superintendent from 2008 to 2016, David, was passionate about educational equity among the students in his district and in comparison to students in major cities across the country.

While David had spent much of his career in the town, he had taken opportunities to see the world. He knew that many of the educators and students in the district hadn't been exposed to schools and communities much beyond the one they were born and raised in. David thought about how he could give his community a sense of pride that they were doing something great for their young people relative to both other school districts in their state and the country.

As early as 2009, David and the associate superintendent were learning how digital content could advance student learning. They knew it would take significant investments in technology across the district to make it truly effective and equal to the best tools and programs available—and not just an add-on to seem like they were staying up to date.

The two of them began a series of informal meetings and door-to-door conversations to educate the community about the need for technology enhancements. Their biggest challenge was convincing a community of mostly retired voters, who didn't have school-age kids in the district, that a bond measure would be necessary. We believe it was through these grassroots efforts, including the consistent and ongoing sharing of information, that a $22 million bond was passed in November 2014.

Within months of approval, the district's team got to work and rallied around their intent to "empower every student and educator to utilize digital tools for high achievement and innovative excellence." The goal was to give every member of the community the best the world has to offer.

The district's leadership team didn't focus on developing a detailed plan; They followed the New Rule to *plan for change, not perfection*. They focused on building the knowledge of each individual. Instead of having people plot out all their action items, they focused on making sure everyone was aligned on the purpose, and they knew each other well enough to be able to appreciate each other's needs. In some ways, they focused on peer empathy. The district didn't have a special projects team to drive this work.

This team included representatives from all of David's departments and more, including school improvement, business and finance, federal programs, human resources, technology, curriculum, arts, and others. His intention was to make sure no one person had all the answers and to guide people to start their learning from different points to ensure there was sharing. Since David knew his community so well, he also knew they may jump to many conclusions quickly. The goal with this approach was to collect new information thoughtfully and analyze it without predetermined notions.

David would often reference the parable "The Blind Men and the Elephant." For this district, the "elephant" was enhancing learning with technology, and David guided people to different parts of the "elephant." One team learned about school models, another team considered digital tools, and another explored professional development. Each time they learned something, they would come together to inform each other and shape their understanding as they continued to feel the different parts of the "elephant."

In January 2015, a month after the bond was approved, there was a kick-off meeting with approximately a hundred people, including every administrator and every school building leader, packed in a crowded cafeteria. Some of the educators there were excited that changes were coming, and others were nervous about the unknown.

David's primary goal for the meeting was to give everyone a sense of why the district strategy for upgrading technology infrastructure would matter to the students and their individual professional careers. He was intent on having all his teachers and staff share the meaning of this message by prioritizing sharing information to inform better decision making.

Historically, as an organization, when they got excited about something they ended up making decisions without access to all of the data. This time around he was focused on making more informed decisions. Teams realized they had to proactively gather the right information. They focused on making sure information was heard and understanding and learning before making decisions in order to ensure that everyone had the best tools and insights to move their work forward. At meetings, they made sure everyone could contribute to the agenda and all voices were heard.

David talked about basketball a lot. He wanted his "players" to be able to do the "no-look pass," which is when a player passes the ball without signaling which direction they plan on passing the ball. The no-look pass requires a team that has practiced together and trusts each other. As an individual, it requires using all your senses to know where all your team-mates are now and where they will be. It seemed that by using transparency, open access to information, and trust building, David built a culture of making things possible and being willing to err on the side of trying and not waiting for the perfect shot.

The approach David wanted to take was to make sure that each team was progressing—the length of the stride could vary, but everyone had to take steps forward. As a leader, that meant he had to make a big change to focus energy on the minimal amount of information people needed versus worrying about getting all the information out to everyone equally and risk overwhelming people.

In the months after the bond measure was approved, the district team worked hard to keep the community engaged so they would continue to support and not derail these efforts. David knew that the success of their implementation required the support of every family, business, politician, and news outlet in town. The communication activities even included placing advertisements in movie theaters, taking out ads on billboards, and conducting town hall–style meetings.

The school district began thinking of itself as moving in one direction and each person figuring out one thing they could do to move toward their vision and to share that with another person. The aim was to create a network of continuous streams of information versus a dam that held back information until it was released at once.

David has moved on to transform another district in the southwest, one that is twice as large and historically high performing. He is there to ensure the district doesn't stagnate. Meanwhile, he has been replaced by a new superintendent, Jack. Though it's common for a new superintendent to come in and change the district's strategy, Jack decided to continue what was in place and move it forward. If the district's teams are communicating and focused on the purpose and process, not the specific programs, why stop the good work that is in motion? With its skill in sharing information and ability to anticipate each other's moves, we believe the school district is set up to implement any program and to experiment with new ideas.

Lessons

As decision-making authority moves from a select few in the C-suite to all roles in an organization, learning better ways of sharing information and transferring knowledge is critical to organizational effectiveness. When communication doesn't take into account the connection between sharers and receivers of information, efforts at transparency can be ineffective and, worse, deepen the divide between people. As we saw with David and the district teams in the case study, effective information sharing needs to be integral to how we get our work done every day *and* how we make our work relevant and connected to our broader communities.

Rather than falling into one of the traps of false transparency, relational transparency is a learned skill. It's the two halves of the New Rule to *harness the flow and let information go*. It takes self-awareness, awareness of the needs of others, and a certain amount of courage, too. We've found a few lessons that can act as helpful guardrails as we develop our skills with sharing—and receiving—the right information at the right time:

- Accept ambiguity.

- Think of others: apply the reverse precautionary principle.

- Ask for what you need: apply the lesson of self-advocacy.

- Plan communication as a process, not an event.

ACCEPT AMBIGUITY

Education leaders always ask Anthony what he believes is the best school model out there, and he always replies that it's the one where each student is learning and each teacher is learning and evolving every day, too. While this answer to the school model question is ambiguous, it provides clarity regarding the ideal experience for students and teachers in an ideal school model.

When our surroundings are changing quickly and assumptions and information are quick to expire, we are constantly working in ambiguity. For senior-level executives, there's a constant navigation between the thirty-thousand-foot and one-hundred-foot

> *What seems complex, conflicting, or confusing can seem less ambiguous when we focus on our purpose and invest in strong processes to guide us through the fog.*

view. What seems complex, conflicting, or confusing can seem less ambiguous when we focus on our purpose and invest in strong processes to guide us through the fog.

A very useful concept is the idea of *known unknowns* and *unknown unknowns,* which comes from Donald Rumsfeld's most famous statement while serving as George W. Bush's secretary of defense:

> *As we know, there are known knowns; there are things we know we know. We also know there are known unknowns; that is to say we know there are some things we do not know. But there are also unknown unknowns—the ones we don't know we don't know. ("Known Knowns," 2006)*

Jack Witlin, former COO of Deloitte Consulting, explained the implication of this concept for leaders with the following two graphics, which he drew on a napkin at an informal lunch. When most people are trying to figure out what they know, don't know, and the unknown, leaders (and team stewards, in the context of responsive school organizations) are able to zoom out see the bigger picture and context affecting the teams or wider organization. Those are the unknown unknowns—the unseen parts of the puzzle (Jack Witlin, personal communication).

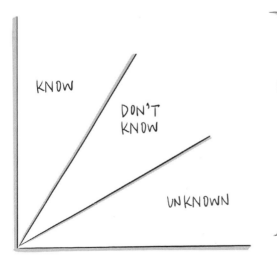

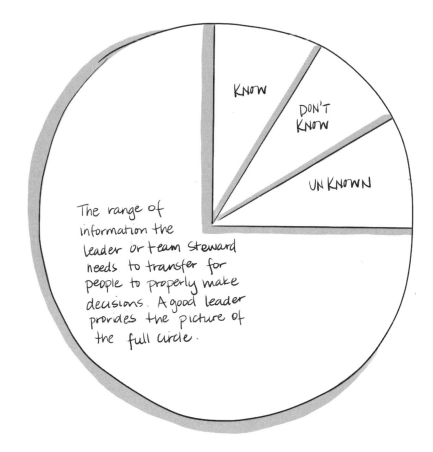

KNOW

DON'T KNOW

UNKNOWN

The range of information the leader or team steward needs to transfer for people to properly make decisions. A good leader provides the picture of the full circle.

This is true for a teacher in a classroom, who has to constantly pursue a better understanding of the big picture for all their students, which might include requirements and opportunities for special programs, academic or social groupings to balance classrooms, or figuring out how to make instruction culturally relevant. A chief academic officer not only stays abreast of current and potential new programs and curricula, but is also uncovering insights about community and national trends on changing workforce needs, gaps in preparation, and developing an evolving and different teacher profile.

Grappling with unknown unknowns requires accepting a degree of ambiguity. Instead of trying to manage all the uncertainty out of a system or team, leaders must accept that we are constantly exploring the unknown unknowns and responding to information as it surfaces.

All of us can invite ourselves and our teams to get comfortable with ambiguity, especially as senior leaders but also as stewards of our roles, and do the following:

1. Publish our goals and thought processes at points along the way to a decision.

2. Bring people together to talk them through decision making after the fact.

3. Use an agreed-upon decision-making process for major decisions so that everyone has a shared language for decisions. You can find one such process outlined in Chapter 4.

You could use one or all three of these strategies in conjunction. Accepting ambiguity leads to a focus on the process, not one magical answer, report, or meeting.

THINK OF OTHERS: APPLY THE REVERSE PRECAUTIONARY PRINCIPLE

The precautionary principle has been applied with great success in the realm of law and policy. It is the principle that taking an action where the ultimate effects are disputed or unknown should be resisted (Science and Environmental Health Network, 2017). For example, if an additive to a food is not well understood and its effects are unclear, then it's best if we don't allow it to be added to our food. It's a simple and powerful notion that can provide direction and safety when there's uncertainty.

However, in a responsive organization, sharing information and transferring knowledge are critical to organizational health. We need to counteract our desire for certainty and complete data with a willingness to experiment. Accepting the unknowns and the potential for unintended consequences, we need to find ways to be much bolder in sharing information, even if we aren't sure how it will be used or we don't think we are ready. We can think of this as the reverse precautionary principle. As we learned in Chapter 4, we need to find ways to *aim for "safe enough to try" instead of consensus.*

> *In a responsive organization, sharing information and transferring knowledge are critical to organizational health. We need to counteract our desire for certainty and complete data with a willingness to experiment.*

A lot of the time we worry about sharing news because it requires context and nuance, which aren't always easy to communicate. As leaders, we have been trained to shield our employees from information that might seem confusing or incomplete. We don't want to create expectations we might not be able to live up to, and we don't want to lead people astray or let our teams down. However, this urge to protect others is rooted in a power dynamic that needn't exist in responsive organizations.

Think about the adage "If you treat someone like a child, they will act like a child." In this case, if you protect people from information that might be incomplete, confusing, or complex, they will continue to expect information to be easy. To build the skill of operating in a complex and ambiguous world, we must take a different approach. Rather than putting precaution ahead of risk, when the effects of information are unknown or debated, the bias should be to share that information and clarify, correct, and expand on it over time.

Recently a school district office worked closely with the local press to get information out to the community about a major new initiative to transform teaching and learning. However, teachers started complaining that they were getting information secondhand through the media. When confronted, the district office offered that they didn't have a lot of the details worked out, nor did they feel they had answers to all the potential questions, so they held back from sharing plans directly with the teaching staff.

Using the New Rule to *harness the flow and let information go*, it would have been better to communicate to the teachers before the press got the information. Instead of waiting until they had a fully delineated plan, the district office could have been honest about saying they agreed on the principles and the staff was getting information as fast as the district office was able to put it together and more information would be released as the project took shape.

This type of imperfection is actually an important part of thinking of others and a model of communication that is relational, not transactional. It aligns with the New Rule of *plan for change, not perfection*. The standard it sets is to communicate a clear purpose and to respond as information is shared. Trust comes from sharing and communication, listening and evolving.

Instead of unveiling the "big plan" and then expecting everyone to jump on board, you can approach information sharing as a partnership and share what you have when you have it in ways that are considerate of the audience. You want to aim for smaller, accessible

> *Aim for smaller, accessible chunks of information to share. You don't want to overcorrect with info dumps and info overload, which are indicative of false transparency.*

chunks of information to share. You don't want to overcorrect with info dumps and info overload, which are indicative of false transparency.

A steady stream of information, presented in formats that are attuned to the audience, lets people absorb ideas over time and take small steps forward. Focusing on the "big plan" is often fear-driven—more a response to our anxieties and desire to have everything "right" than a considerate approach to the needs of the people in our schools and communities. Unintentionally, organizations can be perceived as lethargic and unresponsive when they spend too much time crafting how to share information instead of getting some information out quickly.

ASK FOR WHAT YOU NEED: APPLY THE LESSON OF SELF-ADVOCACY

People struggle with the uneasiness of not being "in the know," not understanding the changes going on around them, the emotional stress of not knowing how to communicate something properly or knowing something while others don't. Our needs around information evoke powerful emotional responses. If we fail to understand that information flow pulls at the emotional core of our being, we will fail to be effective communicators. One important step forward is empowering people to ask and advocate for the information they need.

> *One important step forward is empowering people to ask and advocate for the information they need.*

Rather than second-guessing and ruminating, responsive teams and organizations can work to create cultures where people have permission to ask for what they need—with the understanding that they will get access to it. This takes conscious effort because people keep their insecurities about information to themselves. If you pose the simple question "Well, have you asked for it?" the answer is almost always no. Why? The of fear of speaking out of turn, speaking up to authority figures, or being singled out as "difficult" are the most common reasons we hear.

In the case study, David addressed these insecurities by inviting people from all teams and levels to take part in information-gathering activities. Everyone became an owner, sharer, and receiver of information. He also opened up meeting agendas to address issues from any person, including requests at the meeting. The goal was to break down hierarchies around who was "in the know" and who wasn't.

PLAN COMMUNICATION AS A PROCESS, NOT AN EVENT

To create a positive culture of trust and transparency, we have to become fluent in sharing, listening, responding, and other meaningful forms of engagement that happen over time. We're all affected by the dopamine highs we get from our social media habits. According to a study by RadiumOne (n.d.), "Every time we post, share, 'like,' comment or send an invitation online, we are creating an expectation" of instant gratification (p. 4). We get accustomed to small bursts of news or photos as if those messages can suffice for shared understanding and commitment.

Rather than assuming a message has been transmitted through the kick-off meeting—or a Facebook post or newsletter—David, the superintendent, understood that this first meeting was just the start of a journey. He encouraged people to navigate ambiguity by taking steps forward, however small or large, but just keep moving and sharing learnings to create continuous streams of information versus a dam that held back information until it was released all at once. Externally, the district committed to meaningfully engage the community even after the bond measure was passed. By committing to a long-term relationship with transparency through town halls—and even using billboards to continue to share information—the district was better able to achieve success.

Ongoing communication meant that support and commitment built over time. And the fact that the teachers, staff, district offices, and the whole community all cared lent a sense of urgency and purpose that pushed everyone forward in a positive direction. Even when there were hard moments and unexpected changes, people were ready.

EXPERIMENTS

Experimenting With Sharing Information

Remember: Experiments are designed as trials to be tested out, iterated, studied, and broadly implemented over time. Try out and adapt the experiments on sharing information to fit your role and context.

Getting the right information in the right hands in the right way is essential to a responsive organization. Embracing transparency as a general principle by itself isn't enough and commonly leads to more confusion than clarity. To harness the tidal wave of information in smart ways that support your purpose, try the following experiments.

EXPERIMENT 11

Say "Thank You" for Asking

Culture shapes and is shaped by the small actions and habits of everyday behavior. To create a culture that permits and praises those seeking information, start saying "thank you" to people who dare to clarify, confirm, and ask questions.

- *Clarify:* Encourage and empower each person to ask questions when something isn't clear or there's a sense that more information is needed. If you leave an interaction without requesting the information you need for your role, it's your responsibility alone.

- *Confirm:* Practice confirming what is being communicated whenever there is possible confusion. You can repeat back what you are hearing and confirm that you understand correctly. This simple tool can save a world of trouble later on.

- *Ask questions:* Don't let questions linger and languish. If an issue is relevant to your role, speak up and get the information you need.

- *Most importantly, say "thank you":* Show appreciation for people who pursue and request clarity. When someone uses these tools to get more information from you, make it a point to say "thank you." Clear communications are worth pausing to recognize. And more so, this recognition is a form of encouragement that has a surprisingly profound impact.

One example of how a simple "thank you" can help support culture change comes from the world of healthcare. In 2009, Vanderbilt University Hospital had a hand-washing crisis (Kalb, 2014). Even though hand washing is one of the most effective ways to lessen the spread of infections, a mere fraction of healthcare providers were doing it as often as they needed to. A previous campaign focused on education and monitoring hadn't been effective. So a new strategy was implemented. Between 2009 and 2014, Vanderbilt created a culture of safety with three simple steps that increased hand washing from 58 percent to 97 percent:

1. Empower people with information.

2. Remind each other to wash hands, and say "thank you" if you are reminded.

3. Together, track progress and celebrate when progress is made.

The "thank you" was a critical piece. It created a positive atmosphere to nurture the change. Everyone, including nurses and receptionists, had to be able to remind doctors and senior leaders to wash their hands and trust they would be responded to with appreciation and respect.

When someone, particularly someone less senior than you, clarifies, confirms, or asks for a piece of data, just obliging may not do enough to encourage the behavior to continue. Writing a note or saying in person, "Thank you for asking," reinforces the behavior and creates a positive feedback loop that can help spread the culture of sharing information in your organization.

EXPERIMENT 12
The 3×3 Rule

A common refrain we hear in organizations is "We are data rich but information poor." This idea suggests that data are everywhere, but not communicated in a way that serves people in their roles. With the amount of information we are bombarded with, important information often is missed or arrives when we can't deal with it or are too distracted to engage with it. Plus, in addition to the amount and timing of the information we received, we also are trying to manage the emotions that surround the information being shared.

To make sure that your communications have the best chance of making it across to your audience, you can start following the 3 x 3 rule, which has proved effective in many school and organizational environments. Share things that you want understood three times in three different ways.

In the case study we saw that David's team placed advertisements for their school change initiative in movie theaters, took out ads on billboards, and conducted town hall–style meetings to communicate the new vision for the district. We believe this allowed people to engage with the message multiple times across several different mediums.

Keep in mind that in a digital world, it often helps to combine analog communication tools and experiences with digital ones. For example, let's say you have a meeting where it's decided that teacher leaders will share a piece of important information with their teams. A follow-up to this meeting could include the following steps:

1. Publish three different summaries of the notes (maybe gathered by three different people) in three weekly or biweekly announcement e-mails.

2. Post three posters in the teachers lounge with three different images illustrating one main banner message or caption.

3. Provide three physical cards, each with a different talking point for the main theme of the decision, as a tool school leaders can take with them and hand out to their teams at the next three meetings. This can inform everyone of the purpose and actions for each and the team as a whole.

To think outside the box, hold a brainstorm with your team and get creative. Here are some ideas that have worked for us in the past:

Sampling of Modes of Communication

Medium	Method
Physical visual	Large posters or lettering in a public place
Physical wearable	Buttons, badges, or lanyards communicating the main idea
Physical sharable	Postcards or bookmarks printed for people to pass along

Medium	Method
Digital sharable	An Instagram-style meme with the main idea
Digital visual	A desktop background picture with the key points
Digital tool	An anonymous chat forum that people can log into and ask questions
Digital event	Digital town hall where people can raise questions and get clarity
Interactive virtual or in-person event	Office hours to stop by and visit with the team

Pick three from the list and experiment. To borrow from Chapter 1, instead of picking your three methods and executing blindly, make sure to try each one a few times, reflect on its effectiveness, and iterate as needed. By trying multiple methods you might open up novel communication channels for your most important information.

At first blush, 3 x 3 might seem like overkill, but we can look to Howard Behar, former president of Starbucks, who was known to say at leadership meetings, "You can never get tired of telling the story of what we're doing. People need to hear it over and over again" (personal communication, August 10, 2017).

•••

Sharing Information Is Working When . . .

We are always communicating—whether through our purposeful activities of speaking and e-mailing or through other channels like body language, tone, and even our silence. When we *harness the flow and let information go*, we don't censor or filter information but we do organize and contextualize information so it can be used. Just like in the planning chapter, revisit your commitment to transparency at a regular cadence to celebrate success and refine your efforts.

Information sharing is working when . . .

There is a greater sense of being alive. We spend so much energy worrying about the whole realm of sharing information. Whether it's wondering what we are missing out on, or how to say what needs to be said, or where to find the information we need, communication can be an all-consuming activity. When we can rest confidently in our communication practices and the knowledge that we can find what we need, we spend less energy maneuvering and more energy pursuing our purpose. The whole organization experiments with a greater sense of freedom and aliveness.

Teams and organizations have a clear and motivating purpose. Sharing information leads to clarity, and that clarity leads to a sense of purpose and collective alignment. If information isn't heard or doesn't connect with another person or group, it isn't communication. As we commit to opening communication and increase our skills, we build trust and stay guided by the purpose of our teams and work.

Everyone is continuously evolving, improving, and aiming higher. Sharing information may be one of the hardest parts of our work and personal lives. Yet dealing with this complexity helps us develop the thinking skills and the emotional skills we need to endure and succeed in complex and ambiguous environments. When our schools and districts think about sharing information as a process where we are all continually growing and evolving, it leads to teams and communities where we support each other as we aim higher in sharing, engaging others, and transmitting our feedback, insights, and knowledge.

CHAPTER

6

The Learning Organization

Schools Grow When People Grow

As individuals and within communities of educational champions, for many of us learning is a guiding purpose and probably ranks as one of the most important values in our lives. We value growth, mastery, and multiple intelligences. We value high expectations and perseverance, small steps and breakthroughs. And, it goes without saying, we value the journey of learning as we watch the progress of students over the course of a school year and beyond.

Ironically, while we're immersed in learning environments, many of us have not made a culture of learning for teachers and administrators central to our vision for ourselves and our school communities. Yet we've found over and over again, and research supports, that successful learning isn't about students alone. It's about entire organizations.

A shared learning mindset creates the context for everything we've been talking about in *The NEW School Rules,* from building trust and allowing authority to spread to making decisions "safe enough to try." As Michael Fullan (2004) writes in his book *Leading in a Culture of Change,* "learning in the setting where you work, or learning in context, is the learning with the greatest payoff because it is more specific and because it is social" (p. 126).

> Ironically, while we're immersed in learning environments, many of us have not made a culture of learning for teachers and administrators central to our vision for ourselves and our school communities.

The Problem

Schools and districts face many pressures, among them the drive to get results, mandates to use "proven" solutions, the challenge of multiple initiatives that aren't aligned, and compliance-driven management structures. In the face of these pressures, we can lose our sense of purpose and exist in survival mode. We can miss the excitement and engagement that come with experimenting and innovating, which are intrinsic to learning and learning cultures.

Imagine what it would feel like if professional development were no longer a siloed activity, but an ever-present measure of success embedded in our work every day. Imagine what could be possible if our cultures actually helped ignite educational capacity of our teachers and leaders and the capacity for learning in our classrooms?

"BEST PRACTICES" ARE INHIBITING LEARNING AND INNOVATION

Right now, the ideal of "best practices" to implement and accelerate change is actually preventing schools from meeting the needs of students. Schools are overridden by initiatives that promise results.

The techniques they offer are purported to be proven and widely successful—they are best practices. The concept of best practices implies you don't have to reinvent the wheel with every task, process, and decision. If there are pretested lesson modules, scheduling platforms, student assessments, or staff evaluation tools, why not use them?

As an example, Anthony was in a meeting with a small group of senior administrators in a district in Wyoming who were trying to figure out how Multi-Tiered Systems of Support (MTSS) would align with other initiatives they were working on, like blended learning. A large part of the conversation kept coming back to which initiatives to prioritize. One administrator in particular was stuck on the idea that MTSS was "more proven" and had more "best practices."

Anthony took it as an opportunity to share a different perspective. From his hands-on experience, he'd seen that MTSS is hard to implement, rigid, and, although it can have positive results when implemented well, most people don't enjoy the process.

> Replicating the identical actions from one organization in a completely different organization won't produce the same results.

His argument to the group was as follows: The truth is that many types of initiatives, if supported and implemented well, can produce powerful results. Just because an MTSS effort worked for one site doesn't mean it works for everyone else. Replicating the identical actions from one organization in a completely different organization won't produce the same results.

In reality, best practices are often implemented poorly due to two critical issues:

1. *Best practices are easy to cut and paste into our schools.* That formula consistently fails because the conditions in which a best practice arose somewhere else are different than the situation, time, and place we're dealing with now. Consider something that worked for you that was very personal, like a diet. One diet may work for you, but for someone with a different lifestyle or health situation it may not. School initiatives are no different. Teachers' starting points of experience, relationships, and systems of support are different from school to school.

2. *Best practices are often reduced to one-size-fits-all approaches.*
    Treating best practices as a fixed solution can lead to a com-
    pliance mentality among teachers. The compliance mentality
    prevents teachers from creating and problem solving in the
    classroom, and those are skills that are desperately needed
    to differentiate and personalize learning in the classroom.

Unfortunately, as educators we are fearful of making mistakes. We
rely on best practices to prove a program will work before we
even try. We skip over the fact that the pioneers have found success
with their innovations. Thus it follows that your school or district
has an opportunity to pioneer and innovate techniques rather than
waiting for the next best thing to arrive.

One cognitive problem with best practices or even "success stories" is located in the notion of *adaptive emulation*, where actors
respond to perceived failure by imitating their most successful
peers (Strang & Macy, 2001). A classic example is the experience of the Finnish cell phone giant Nokia, which dominated the
competition with a 41 percent share of the market in 2007. Seven
years later, during a press conference announcing Nokia's acqui-
sition by Microsoft, and really its demise as an industry leader,
Nokia CEO Stephen Elop ended his speech saying, "We didn't do
anything wrong, but somehow, we lost." Upon saying that, all his
management team, himself included, teared up (Gupta, 2016). The

sad thing about what the CEO said is that they did do something wrong, which was not learning and not evolving based on the changes in the market.

Organizations that pioneer best practices, instead of waiting for them, are constantly learning and evolving. For these organizations, best practices are standard practices, which continue to improve and continue to get more attuned to the current needs of students and staff.

> *Organizations that pioneer best practices, instead of waiting for them, are constantly learning and evolving.*

THERE ISN'T LEARNING WITHOUT LISTENING

According to Harvard Business School professor Francesca Gino, organizations are impeded by the fear of failure, insufficient reflection, believing that we need to conform, and inadequate frontline involvement in addressing problems (Gino, & Staats, 2015). Companies of all types are working hard to be nimble and attract the best talent. Cutting-edge organizations are cultivating the New Rule to *plan for change, not perfection* in all aspects of their work. They value continuous improvement and iteration, so they can adjust quickly to new information and an unpredictable future. They are employing strategies like Stanford University psychologist Carol Dweck's work on the *growth mindset* to continue to develop and engage younger generations. They're moving away from a management focus on the company to one focused on the customer. Just consider how companies like Starbucks and Apple engage and delight the customer with continuous iteration of their products and creating wonderful places to linger and shop. This all requires listening, learning, and change.

As school systems begin to move their discussions from maintaining and sustaining the education system based on past needs to more student-centered models, they also need to become more responsive as their students—and the world around them—change at a pace faster than most current school systems can support.

At a recent meeting, Bror Saxberg, the vice president for learning science at the Chan Zuckerberg Initiative, gave the example of his father, who is a professor at the University of Washington. His father started to realize that teaching had changed when his students would immediately validate and question the case studies he was presenting by doing Google searches during his lectures. He couldn't stick to the point he wanted to make with the example. Instead, he had to be much more flexible and responsive to new information coming at him from the students.

THE MINDSET OF EFFICIENCY

In a small town in upstate New York around the Finger Lakes, a school district is making a big shift to personalized learning. At a kick-off meeting where a team representing different members of the district was formed, there was a gentleman sitting quietly, with his arms crossed. He was engaged but had a look of reservation. When he was asked directly if he had any questions, his initial answer was no. When that was followed up with some gentle probing about whether he was nervous about the work, he answered an immediate yes. He explained that he joined the team to better understand how much work was going to be involved in pursuing this new direction in the district. It turned out he was also the union president. The ensuing discussion brought into the open the fact that a shift in direction would indeed be a challenging and intensive undertaking.

We all know that learning and changing brings with it more work than simply maintaining the status quo. The question for the school district was: If through this work the teachers would feel more engaged and appreciated, would it be worth the effort? Absolutely, the union leader and team agreed.

Investing time and resources to unlearn and relearn mindsets, skills, and behaviors is not always the most efficient route. In fact, failure is expected because it takes time, focus, and practice to develop fluency and muscle memory. If we focus on efficiency, learning is minimal. In fact, it can easily become mindless. Instead, in a world where we are constantly navigating new information, we should focus on how we can learn most effectively so that we can work most effectively.

> If we focus on efficiency, learning is minimal.

The New Rule

Schools Grow When People Grow

Learning organizations are environments that continually move individuals and teams toward higher levels of learning. Learning functions as an engine for evolution and growth. Learning is the living, breathing, growing part of our roles and cultures that brings our work to life.

When schools follow the New Rule that *schools grow when people grow*, we understand that genuine learning must happen for the adults and the students. A learning mindset—and a bias for higher-order thinking—energizes everyone and leads to bigger gains in skills, creativity, and engagement.

> *A learning mindset—and a bias for higher-order thinking—energizes everyone and leads to bigger gains in skills, creativity, and engagement.*

In the model of Bloom's Taxonomy there are six levels of learning:

1. *Remembering:* The learner is able to recall, restate, and remember information.

2. *Understanding:* The learner is able to explain ideas and concepts of the information.

3. *Applying:* The learner is able to make use of the information in a situation outside of where it was learned.

4. *Analyzing:* The learner is able to deconstruct the information to gain deeper understanding of the parts.

5. *Evaluating:* The learner makes decisions based on in-depth reflection and justification.

6. *Creating:* The learner creates new ideas and information using what was previously learned.

Just as we want students to learn and operate at the higher levels of thinking and learning according to Bloom's Taxonomy, the organization needs to operate at those levels, too. Schools that focus primarily on adopting and implementing programs and initiatives that others have created are operating at the levels of remembering and understanding. A more valuable approach to take learning to the next level would be evaluating and iterating on best practices for real and sustained success.

Think about the story of the Nokia CEO. His statement, "We didn't do anything wrong, but somehow, we lost," says it all. They were operating at levels of remembering and understanding versus evaluating and creating. If they had spent more time at the higher-order levels of thinking and learning, they would have been more innovative.

We can recognize a learning organization, team, or individual when these things happen:

- New ideas and opportunities are brought forward and new work is "spawned." If new things aren't percolating—from the ground up as well as from senior leadership—it's the clearest sign that the organization isn't learning and isn't feeling alive, creative, and innovative.

- People are having difficult discussions. Yes, indeed. We want to see people caring enough to share tensions and problems, ideally in constructive ways in team settings, not simply as gossip in halls and lunchrooms. Learning and creating is hard work; it can be uncomfortable and scary because it taps into the unknown.

- Failure and learning are being shared openly. When you ask someone what happened to an initiative or project, they are comfortable enough to say, "It didn't work, so we went in another direction" or "We discovered something we didn't expect and decided to change course."

- Meetings are an opportunity to learn together. After each meeting you feel you received the information or clarity you needed to take another step forward.

Case Study: Leadership Capacity Building

This mostly urban school district lies in the northeast, where historically manufacturing and engineering were core to the local economy. In the 1970s, the city's unemployment rate started to peak as manufacturing declined. By the 2000s, educational institutions became the number one and two employers in the area: the city's university and public school district. Yet in 2012 the public schools and students were in distress. A report by the school district administration and the teachers association found that 84 percent of the students qualified for free or reduced-price lunch, 96 percent of the students attended underperforming schools, 51 percent of the students graduated on time, and district students accounted for 85 percent of youth incarcerated in the county.

Between 2012 and 2016, the school district not only put together many different plans to improve education but also contracted with numerous outside firms to execute on elements of this work.

In April 2015, the district's senior cabinet met to discuss yet one more approach to turning around the worst-performing schools in the district. Many of the previous consultant-led initiatives had showed initial promise but were not working out. Schools were labeled "persistently struggling" by the state due to consistently low test scores.

The district cabinet seemed to be visibly suspect of yet another change effort. The tension in the meeting I attended was palpable as attendees avoided the proverbial elephant in the room. With some prodding and the willingness to have honest conversations, one of the participants finally raised the point that many consultants had come to the district with big promises but left with little measurable success after wasting lots of the leadership's time.

Other people started to chime in. Outside experts got plenty of resources allocated to them, they said, but internal staff members were being shortchanged. They were asked to educate the consultants on their issues yet none of the resources were being invested in them. Here they were at the start of a new initiative with a new team of experts coming in to help. They felt the superintendent and the school board should focus on investing in the people who invested their lives and careers in the district. They wanted help to learn and grow themselves instead of hiring so-called experts to tell them all the things they were doing wrong.

These frank comments appeared to set up a turning point for this committed but discouraged team. In fact, a new approach had been envisioned for these struggling schools. Patricia, the chief academic officer, who had extensive experience building internal capacity in other districts, had already decided to focus on school leadership development.

Rather than deploying a new consultant or new program to "transform" these schools, the new approach sought to build relationships between the district administration and school-level leaders. It allowed schools to explore a broad range of instructional strategies and aligned district supports like coaching to specific needs in the schools. The outside consultants wouldn't be set up in a plan-and-control role. They would help design and implement an initial *minimal viable plan*—or MVP—and together the schools and consultants would take a team-based plan-and-evolve approach. The school leaders would bring their knowledge back to their own teams, schools, and classrooms to make the changes themselves and refine them as they saw what worked.

The district administrative team was able to give this new approach a fair chance. As they participated in more and more workshops and worked alongside the school leaders, they started to see small successes. But the big shift came in 2016, just a year later, when the "persistently struggling" designation was lifted.

With this capacity-building approach, the reform plan was launched in the district's ten historically worst-performing schools. The team understood that failure in these schools couldn't be any worse, so with the *aim for "safe enough to try" instead of consensus* rule firmly in mind, they felt confident enough to try new things and experiment as they went. Within twelve months, these ten schools started to see dramatic changes. Not only were measures of academic growth improving at a faster rate than at the other schools in the district, but the students, teachers, and building staff were also visibly more energized and engaged.

The school leadership had new confidence that change was possible and saw that even small steps had big ripple effects. Creativity was pushed into the classrooms, and teaching methods were exciting and fresh. Teachers sparked dialogues with students about what was working for them and what was not, leading to strong feedback loops and openness to mistakes, innovations, and change. If a new type of curriculum, technique, or technology wasn't working, they would try something else. Conversations were changing, too. What started as small nodes of change within each school spread across more school teams and classrooms with numerous pilot projects and lots of learning from each other. For some of the principals, it was hard making sure they weren't running too fast.

The school district was discovering in real time the New Rule that *schools grow when people grow*. Teachers and staff appeared to be evolving from a model of trying to remember and understand everything they were told to creating and evaluating the innovations they were making. The teams and schools didn't do everything from scratch. There were visits to other school districts, and they borrowed elements of models they liked at schools with similar conditions. But the exciting part was that they had more insight into what their needs were, chose more relevant solutions, and were able to adapt new solutions to their specific needs.

Building capacity seems to have been hugely meaningful for the district's schools and the community. Recently, the district has made visible moves demonstrating trust in its people. First, a thirty-three-year employee of the district became the next superintendent of the district. Another employee, who also spent her whole thirty-three-year career in the district, is now the chief academic officer. They are making other changes in the district to adapt to a new frame of mind toward being an organization that can evolve and grow from within. They've created new roles to support the initial ten turnaround schools and continue to add new waves of schools to undergo this mindset shift from being told what best practices to use to developing and implementing their own best practices for others to learn from.

Lessons

LESSON

You surely have heard this famous quote attributed to Albert Einstein: "The definition of insanity is doing the same thing over and over again and expecting different results." Sanity means we have to try new things.

If we want our students to learn and grow, we need to learn and grow. When schools and districts begin to learn, innovate, and evolve, then all the people in the organization learn, innovate, and evolve at an accelerated pace.

Here are a few big picture lessons that can help you think about your own and your organization's learning environment:

- Use the physical environment to build a learning environment.

- Promote optimal zones of learning (for adults as well, not just kids).

- Develop a learning mindset: the stance of agent, not subject.

- Face the truth.

USE THE PHYSICAL ENVIRONMENT TO BUILD A LEARNING ENVIRONMENT

All organizations create environments that push people to behave in similar ways. Each person may have a different starting point or degree of alignment with the behaviors that define the organization, but as a whole, the organization attracts and keeps people that have similar biases. Thus, if we want to create learning environments for our students—which we do!—we need to create organizations and structures that are biased toward learning.

Anthony met Greg, the former superintendent of a Southern California school district, through a leadership awards fellowship program. Greg invited Anthony to attend the opening of a new high school in his district.

Beyond having buildings that were laid out to support open classrooms and learning in and outside of the classroom, the district realized that many teachers had never experienced a career outside of education, so it started a summer internship program for teachers to work in local businesses, like Sun City. These workplaces functioned as new environments, which spawned new ways of thinking and doing things.

At the new high school, how they think about school has evolved into a learning community. They changed their physical understanding of a school as an open campus where classrooms extend inside and outside to a patio area (of course, the mild climate helps make that possible), social spaces, and classrooms with open doors and big windows. They changed their understanding of the work of a teacher by pushing teachers to teach multiple subjects in one class and engaging them in professional development that allows them to truly understand the workforce outside of education. By breaking the large organization into smaller units and teams, the school enabled those to learn and act faster and solve problems more quickly.

PROMOTE OPTIMAL ZONES OF LEARNING (FOR ADULTS AS WELL, NOT JUST KIDS)

Learning, by definition, means failing—often and frequently. We have to remind ourselves that if we didn't fail while learning, we wouldn't be challenging ourselves enough. The *zone of proximal development* is a concept that was developed by the influential Russian psychologist Lev Vygotsky in the early 1930s. Over several generations his work has been an important foundation for the theory of cognitive development and concept of *scaffolding* of learning.

The zone of proximal development is defined as the difference (gap) between a child's actual developmental level, as determined by independent problem solving, and the child's potential level of development, as determined through problem solving under adult guidance or in collaboration with more capable peers. In fact, the concept is the essential definition of *tension*, which we defined in Chapter 2 as "the gap between what is and what could be, or what we wish it to be."

> We have to remind ourselves that if we didn't fail while learning, we wouldn't be challenging ourselves enough.

Lev Vygotsky's Model of Cognitive Development

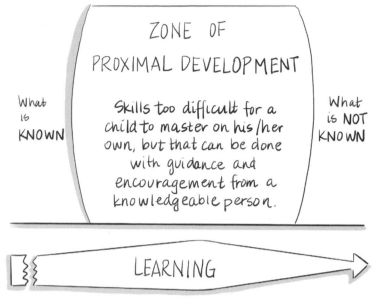

ZONE OF
PROXIMAL DEVELOPMENT

What
is
KNOWN

Skills too difficult for a
child to master on his/her
own, but that can be done
with guidance and
encouragement from a
knowledgeable person.

What
is NOT
KNOWN

LEARNING

McLeod (2012).

This gap between where we are and where we want to be is often a source of stress or even fear. When we worry that we haven't figured "it" out yet, or that we have not attained mastery, we can feel "less than." However, the zone of proximal development suggests that leaning into this sweet spot with guidance and encouragement is exactly where we should be.

For students, this guidance and encouragement comes from teachers, counselors, parents, specialists, and more capable peers. For adults, cognitive development can come from more experienced peers, training, formal education, coaching and mentoring, supportive feedback, and problem solving with peers where tensions are resolved and new solutions are crafted.

This guidance and encouragement can also include support and collaboration available on the Internet with online courses, YouTube videos, and connected networks like Facebook, LinkedIn, and Twitter. Guidance can be represented by a useful short comment, and a "like" or "thumbs up" can represent encouragement. This type of support is now available globally, and the level of expertise—and enthusiasm (likes)—that can be accessed is limitless. We aren't relying on encouragement from one individual, but from a crowd.

THE NEW SCHOOL RULES

Leveraging this rich, multifaceted universe of support to address our fears of not knowing or feeling that we don't "get it" can help us stretch our optimal zone of learning. With practice, over time we can transform our fear into curiosity and excitement, allowing ourselves to stretch beyond what we may have thought possible.

What if the gap between where you are and where you could be actually inspired you instead of frightened you? What if you understood your zone of proximal development and the types of guidance and encouragement you need most?

> *What if the gap between where you are and where you could be actually inspired you instead of frightened you?*

DEVELOP A LEARNING MINDSET: THE STANCE OF AGENT, NOT SUBJECT

We have a tendency to focus on the outward signs of leadership—confidence, communication, and influence—but we've learned that truly transformational organizations are led at all levels by people who are willing to engage in inward transformation.

Having worked with hundreds of individuals and organizations with all kinds of personalities, strengths, and experiences, we know just how unique each of us is. We have unique motivations, histories, skills, and passions. Yet there is one important distinction that shines through when we look at people who are learning and those who are stagnating:

- Those who are stagnating view themselves as *subjects*; they feel they are being acted upon by the organization.

- Those who are learning view themselves as *agents*; they see themselves as actors or directors in charge of extracting learning from their work experiences, and they believe they have the power to influence the organization.

How do these ways begin to show up?

Someone who takes the subject approach is much more likely to talk about the organization as a monolithic enterprise, with its own biases and shortcomings. This person is more likely to blame the organization for challenges. The subject-oriented person says things like this:

"They don't do a good enough job of engaging me."

"This team is terrible at feedback—so I'm not learning anything."

"The organization's strategy is constantly changing; they don't know what they are doing."

On the other hand, the person who takes the agent approach is more likely to include themselves in their observations and see themselves taking an active role in trying to shape the culture around them. The agent-oriented person may say things like this:

"I need to schedule a time to sit down with my manager and put together a professional development plan. I feel like I'm not progressing as fast as I'd like."

"I'm working on modeling this new approach with my teams to see if it helps shift the culture."

In the case study, we saw how the school district moved from simply executing on a consultant's plan to focusing on leadership development and learning at the school level. We believe it was through this shift that people felt empowered to begin experimenting and innovating at their schools. School-based teams were leading change and evolving strategies based on tight feedback loops with students. This mindset shift, from relying on someone else to fix your problems to being an agent in your own development, is key to organizational change.

As individuals and organizations, we can move to create developmental cultures that allow people to look inward and develop a sense of curiosity and enthusiasm for tackling internal transformation and learning. At the same time, we can help people get clear around the kind of support they need to deal effectively with challenges and discomfort and how to grow not only in their skills and technical abilities but in their ability to communicate and lead.

Our personal resistance can often be a clue to our own edge of learning. One company's vice president had a wake-up call when he called Alexis to say, "I am uncomfortable with how fast this is all rolling out. It feels like a lot of this work is involving my people and I don't have control over it."

To this Alexis asked a few questions:

"Do you need to feel comfortable with this change?"

"Is being comfortable a prerequisite for change in your organization?"

"Is there some value you feel we are missing out on that's giving rise to these worries?"

"Is there something to learn in embracing what is uncomfortable?"

These questions reframed the issues and led to insights about what was really at play. This leader wasn't sure his role was adding value to the organizational change and was worried that he would lose legitimacy within the organization. He was able to come up with a plan to help him address his own insecurities and find a way to be active in his own development.

Scenarios like this show up for all of us in dozens of ways and sometimes multiple times in a day. We're each on an internal developmental journey, especially as we increase our bias for higher-order thinking. A beginning learner wants to be told and handed learning opportunities. An advanced learner or agent finds learning in everything and is able to see challenges as an opportunity to reflect and grow.

FACE THE TRUTH

The school district in the case study seemed to be able to start on the journey to improvement with a simple act of honesty. The moment when the cabinet team stopped being silent subjects and opened up about how consultants hadn't worked for them allowed the effort to move forward on solid footing. The journey toward greater learning starts with being truthful—even when it's uncomfortable.

> *The journey toward greater learning starts with being truthful—even when it's uncomfortable.*

Another way that the district demonstrated its willingness to face the truth was the shift to being open to student feedback. By opening up to receive insight and data from multiple sources, including students as valuable human sensors, it was better able to build an accurate picture of its schools. Knowing its schools well enough meant the district could adapt and refine practices to address the unique needs of each school.

In order to experience true growth, as an individual, a team, or an entire organization, you have to begin with the truth. A leadership development plan that doesn't start with a deep understanding of each individual's strengths and weaknesses is pointless. And a school improvement plan that doesn't begin with an honest conversation about what has and hasn't worked won't gain traction. These moments of facing the truth may be difficult and downright awkward for some individuals, but if we are to engage in the work of necessary change, we have to see them as growth opportunities. The chance to challenge ourselves to become stronger, more courageous agents of change begins with the simple but radical conviction that *schools grow when people grow.*

....

Experimenting With Learning

Remember: Experiments are designed as trials to be tested out, iterated, studied, and broadly implemented over time. Try out and adapt the experiments on learning organizations to fit your role and context.

Most schools and districts have a set of beliefs about the values of learning, embracing failure, and developing people. But until those beliefs and practices are infused in the organization rather than siloed in professional development days and activities, we won't have true learning organizations.

As Ray Dalio, founder of the world's largest hedge fund, Bridgewater Associates, wrote in a company-wide e-mail, "Do you worry more about how good you are or about how fast you are learning?" If we truly believe that *schools grow when people grow,* it is self-evident that we'll make learning one of the essential measures of success for everything we do.

Here we offer three experiments to try to become a better learning organization.

EXPERIMENT 13

Start a Reflection Practice

We can't navigate a course of learning if we don't take time to reflect. As Confucius said, "Learning without reflection is a waste. Reflection without learning is dangerous."

You probably already engage in some reflection. Replaying a difficult conversation or thinking through the way a meeting played out are natural ways our mind processes events. However, in order for "reflection to be meaningful, it must be metacognitive, applicable, and shared with others" (MindShift, 2014, para. 1). Metacognition is thinking about one's thinking or, in this case, learning.

An authentic reflection practice takes time because it requires that you connect with your weaknesses as well as your strengths and embrace sometimes difficult truths about yourself.

Over time, the goal is to reflect to better understand what to do next, which means testing and refining one's observations to see if they fit, if they are true, if they are applicable.

Effective reflection isn't a solitary pursuit. We need to share our reflections to get feedback from others and to continue to learn and grow.

To begin a reflection practice, start small. Find a discreet area you want to evaluate and develop, whether that's building rapport with people on your team, making more engaging presentations, or reviewing your communication strategies with families. Here is a four-step approach to experiment with reflection:

1. Set an intention to learn.
2. Act, observe, and reflect using the SWOT approach.
3. Gather feedback.
4. Make changes.

1. Set an intention to learn.

It might sound counterintuitive to reflect on the future, but it is important to develop an internal compass and starting point for learning. Until you have more practice, your initial reflections might be short and sweet and as simple as setting up priorities for the day. You could ask yourself, "What do I want to accomplish today?" or "What do I want to learn from this project?" If you've used a Franklin Covey planner, David Allen's Getting Things Done method, or other models, you're familiar with the fact that these tools all involve some form of reflection about one's purpose, goals, and thinking processes. These insights become guideposts for your learning.

For an initial experiment, you might have the intention of learning to communicate more effectively. To structure your reflection, you can create a simple rubric to evaluate yourself against the attributes of a strong communicator in a responsive school or district setting. A rubric will help you focus your reflection.

Sample Rubric for Attributes of a Strong Communicator

Characteristic to Reflect on and Develop	Description
Listen and ask questions	Seek to understand before being understood. Clarify, confirm, and ask questions.
Share data	Data should be simple, concise, specific—not rambling or tangential.
Push work toward clarity	Pinpoint which role has authority to move work forward. Capture action items.

2. Act, observe, and reflect using the SWOT approach.

Once you've reflected and set a clear intention, take action. In this case you would bring your reflections into a particular meeting and use them as a guidepost and reminder of the approach you are trying to take.

After the meeting, your mind will likely begin to replay your interactions. Formalize your reflection by sitting down with your rubric and capturing notes on how well you performed in each area. If you don't have a rubric, a tried-and-true structure for reflection is a SWOT analysis, which identifies *strengths, weaknesses, opportunities,* and *threats*.

Let's say you made a budget presentation to the regional leadership team. Afterward, your SWOT might cover the following:

- Strengths: *What did you do well in the presentation compared to what you expected?* Maybe you got a few laughs with a story you told. Maybe people were really excited about the topic and wanted to contribute.

- Weaknesses: *What were some gaps or areas for improvement in your presentation?* Perhaps you were speaking too quickly because of time limitations and the amount of content you planned to cover. Or your handouts or PowerPoint may have been crowded with information and as a result too hard for people to read and understand.

- Opportunities: *What can you leverage in the future?* Maybe you spent too much time preparing material you didn't need or use. Looking ahead, you see you can reduce the amount of work you need to put into certain parts of your presentation.

- Threats: *What conditions could cause trouble in the future?* Your boss or executive team may not be on board with the changes you're experimenting with, a signal that you need to explain and get their support for your approach.

A rubric and SWOT analysis are just two of many ways you can structure your reflection. What's important here is to have a process to move the internal conversation in your head to an external place where you capture your thoughts in a way that is concrete and sharable.

3. Gather feedback.

In addition to your own analysis, getting the broadest set of data to inform your plan of action means asking for—and receiving—useful feedback. You can't rely on "no news is good news" and assume everything you're doing is great. People are often reluctant to provide meaningful feedback because it's easier to say "great job" and move on. Vague, open-ended requests put all responsibility on the feedback provider.

To flip this dynamic, do your reflection first and then ask others to affirm, edit, or challenge your insights. For example, instead of asking, "How did I do?" if you've done a SWOT or variation of one, you can ask something specific. You

> *Instead of asking, "What feedback does anyone have for me?" ask, "What advice does anyone have for me?"*
>
> *—Claire Lew, CEO of Know Your Company*

might say, "I think I went into too much detail on this topic. Do you think I reached the audience? What would you have changed?" This will lead to concrete plans for action that you can measure against your original reflections.

Claire Lew (2017), the CEO of Know Your Company, suggests one simple change to unlock more honest feedback. Instead of asking, "What feedback does anyone have for me?" ask, "What advice does anyone have for me?" People are more likely to oblige when they feel like you value their opinion and take them seriously.

4. Make changes.

Translating your reflections into action brings learning to fruition. As you review your SWOT and feedback, you'll want to test and put your insights into action. Pick one thing to change the next time you are up for a presentation, and continue the pattern of reflection, practice, reflection, and feedback, ultimately creating an ongoing cycle of learning.

EXPERIMENT 14
Create a Habit of Learning Every Day

We often talk about wanting to learn, but we believe we don't have enough time or long enough blocks of open time to make any real learning possible. Organizations have tried to address this time squeeze with programs like professional learning communities (PLCs) or even providing employees with opportunities to take online courses of their choosing through websites like Lynda.com, but unfortunately these efforts aren't effective in building learning organizations. As one-off programs they can contribute to teacher and staff development, but they don't build habits and routines that promote a mindset and bias toward learning. To truly become a learning organization, you have to develop a collective mindset and fluency in learning every day. Learning doesn't have to be in big blocks of time. It can truly happen in fifteen to thirty minutes a day.

Research from Benjamin Bloom (1984) and John Hattie (2012) shows that more learning happens when the learner receives immediate feedback versus learning in isolation. In fact, Bloom found that tutorial style learning, where a tutor can be assigned to two or three learners, followed by feedback procedures, increased learning growth by 95 percent. Even in small daily bursts, when small groups of learners can provide feedback and collaborate on a topic, it increases learning growth at almost twice the rate of learning in a silo.

Here are some tips and prompts to get you started:

- Subscribe to an online journal or newsletter in your area of expertise that covers new research, social and global issues, or other related ideas that go beyond the usual tips and advice. Ideally, it publishes a substantive new article or a round-up of articles at least once a week. (An alternate approach, or a complementary one, might be a weekly screening of a TED or TEDx Talk in such categories as education, psychology, leadership, science, or related topics.)

- After reading the article, write a short reflection:
  - How does this apply to a conversation I had recently?
  - How does this inform a project I'm involved in?
  - Who was struggling with a similar issue?

- Send the article and your relevant reflection to a learning partner or a relevant peer, which will generate a dialogue. To be a learning organization, it has to be a two-way activity. Everyone needs to create learning opportunities and actively participate in learning moments.

EXPERIMENT 15

Personal Portfolios

In responsive organizations everyone is a steward of their roles, challenges, and personal growth. We're used to thinking of great managers as those bosses and mentors who push us to fulfill our potential. But what would it mean if everyone were capable of doing this for themselves? Instead of waiting for formal development opportunities to be doled out by your manager, take your development into your own hands, starting with the data you collect about your goals, successes, and areas you have identified in your reflection practice.

Regardless of the current formal processes in your organization for reviews and development plans, you can start by creating your portfolio. Start today by creating one physical folder and one digital folder where you capture and collect electronic feedback, artifacts from projects you've worked on, and your own reflections and assessments throughout the year. Periodically make notes on your achievements, growth, and areas for improvement.

Schedule a recurring time to meet with your manager, mentor, or peer partner to review your portfolio, share your reflections, and discuss growth and goals. You'll be surprised at the incremental growth you experience by this simple practice. The portfolio process also has an important side benefit— by the time the formal review process takes place, you will already have an understanding of your development and feedback won't come as a surprise.

The portfolio process is also a powerful tool for developing our ability to give and receive feedback. In keeping with the emphasis on all kinds of data in responsive organizations, one of the most important pieces of data you can gather is personal feedback. In fact, your portfolio is only as good as the quality of feedback in it. The feedback we currently use might be limited to our managers or through formal channels like our annual review process. Even if we proactively reach out for feedback from our peers and teams, the response on average is not specific or actionable. Use the insights in Experiment 13 to ask the right questions and get meaningful feedback.

With a personal portfolio, you have an accurate representation of your skills, areas for development, and ideas for where you might step into new levels of responsibility or areas of work. You can think of it as a tool to help you lean into your zone of proximal development—stretching yourself in receiving advice and feedback, becoming more effective, and taking risks. One concrete application of a portfolio can be to help you "pitch" yourself when you see a new role that you'd like to step into. Coming prepared with a concise summary of your goals, strengths, and growth priorities can help you convey a clear picture of your value to a new role or project. Not only does this help build the skill of self-advocacy, but it also serves the organization by connecting opportunities with latent talent.

The overarching purpose of a portfolio is to shift ownership for development and growth to individuals as the stewards of their roles and learning. Each action encourages a culture of leadership development for everyone, supporting the potential that resides in all of us.

The Learning Organization Is Working When . . .

In 2013, Katrina Fried wrote a *Huffington Post* article titled "21 Reasons to Quit Your Job and Become a Teacher," which was shared widely. These are her first three reasons:

1. To encourage children to dream big

2. To positively impact the future of our world

3. To live with a deep sense of purpose

They are so powerful because they remind us that if teachers want to help students achieve their dreams, teachers have to have a path to achieve their dreams. Learning organizations help grow dreams, impact, and sense of purpose by enhancing—and valuing—the learning of everyone. A learning organization is working when . . .

There is a greater sense of being alive. Learning is like breathing. It's natural and gives you a reason to strive and grow. When you are part of a learning organization, you regularly experience a mixture of excitement and fear—a sure sign that you are pushing your zone of proximal development. Just like an organism, there is continual reshaping and evolution. While some may say this is unstable and too ambiguous, the learning organization embraces this process of new growth and necessary endings. Every day feels fresh, slightly unpredictable, and even exhilarating because, in fact, the future is unpredictable.

Teams and organizations have a clear and motivating purpose. There's so much out there now that can distract us and take our time. To stay motivated to learn, the organization's purpose has to be profound and clear. Learning takes effort, and it can feel risky, hard, unpredictable, and nonlinear, especially when we try to reach higher levels of learning, generate new solutions, and transfer learning to others.

Everyone is continuously evolving, improving, and aiming higher. Individuals not only have a purpose that is aligned with the greater mission, but they each know how they contribute. Once they are engaged in the purpose, everyone is challenging themselves to improve their current skills, learn new ones, and evolve to new levels of expertise. The key word in this is *everyone*—even managers and supervisors are able to approach work with a beginner's mind, the Zen Buddhist concept introduced by Shunryu Suzuki (1970) in the first line of his most famous book: "In the beginner's mind there are many possibilities, but in the expert's there are few" (p. 1). With expertise, you realize how much you don't know. The aim is to cultivate the curious beginner's mind of the child, of the person full of wonder, of the expert who knows just how much they don't know and how valuable it is to be open to new ideas, people, data, and even problems. A mindset and culture of learning reminds us to value what we don't know just as much as what we do know. It's the path of continual discovery balanced with the humility for all we do not yet know.

••

A Responsive Roadmap

Beginning the Shift to New Organizational Practices

Now that you've read through the six building blocks for responsive organizations, you're probably wondering how to begin. How do you go beyond small, one-time experiments on your own or with your immediate team colleagues? How do you actually begin to apply the principles and experiments in this book to manifest real change?

In this section we share the following:

- the three dimensions of change you'll want to be alert to as you experiment
- a plan for implementation with an adaptable five-step Responsive School Roadmap to sequence your experiments with these new organizational practices

THREE DIMENSIONS OF CHANGE

Whenever we make changes in our work or lives, we wonder if we're doing the right thing, if we're doing it in the best way, and if the changes we're making are truly making a difference. Perspective helps.

Awareness of three dimensions of change helps demystify a process that can be anxiety producing or just confusing. Here are three dimensions to pay attention to as you implement the New Rules of responsive organizations:

1. *Individual, independent change:* Any one of us can become more responsive in our work. Regardless of the current organizational structure and practices of your school or district, many of the mindset shifts and a number of the experiments we recommend can happen independently, while others work well together. Think of atoms and molecules. Atoms can exist independently, while molecules are atoms bonded together to create a complex organism or, in the case of organizations, a complex behavior. Start where you can, based on your roles, experience, team willingness, and the larger culture of your organization.

2. *Group adoption, habit building, and deepening of change:* While the principles of responsive organizations can start with, and are ultimately owned by, each person as the steward of their role, it is through broad adoption that change becomes embedded in the DNA of a team or a whole organization. When habits spread it creates a network effect, accelerating awareness and a "new normal" for how things are done. If everyone is doing it, I'll do it too. For example, the practice of "defaulting to yes" may start with one or a few people, but with continuous effort and reminders from team members, the practice becomes a phrase everyone uses and a new way of working together. However, even then, it may take ongoing review and renewed commitment over time to maintain the integrity and underlying intent of the practice.

   Donella Meadows (2008), the systems guru and author of *Thinking in Systems,* wrote, "If you want to understand the deepest malfunctions of systems, pay attention to the rules and who has power over them" (p. 158). As part of this second dimension of change, identifying the rule makers and engaging and enlisting them in your experiments for change can have a profound impact on the entire structure of your system. Challenge your team to grow and evolve together. This requires a deep commitment to facing the truth, recognizing ingrained mental models and behaviors, and building new habits.

3. *Continuous learning, evolution, and iteration:* As you begin to practice habits and experiment with change, you will experiment with certain decisions and protocols and you might feel "We did it!" effectively crossing off that responsive practice from your to-do list. There's some truth in this. When identifying a strong, aligned purpose for your team or district, you don't want to get lost in constant rethinking and change. You need to stick with practices for them to become real habits and a culture of change. Your team might adopt a meeting protocol, and we suggest not tweaking it too often. It's a balancing act. If you jump too fast to make changes before you've given your practice or goal the time needed to change your behavior, you will continue to jump to the next "shiny object" looking for magic bullets.

On the other hand, once something is working, that doesn't mean it will work forever. Just as our organizations need to be alive, engaged, and responsive, our practices need to be alive and open to revisiting and change over time to keep them relevant and meaningful. We need to revisit them on a regular cadence. Remember that team members, roles, protocols, tools, and every other system feature that might have been right at one point may be wrong at another.

These three dimensions of change—individual-level practices, collective-level habits, and an ongoing inclination to evolve, iterate, and grow—work together to create responsive organizations that feel stimulating, exciting, and alive.

INDIVIDUAL   COLLECTIVE   ON-GOING EVOLUTION

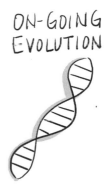

A PLAN FOR IMPLEMENTATION

It can be helpful to imagine the actual flow of how these changes can be introduced and how they might take hold over time. This roadmap can be used as-is or, ideally, adapted to your stage and needs. As we discussed in Chapter 6 and elsewhere, the more you can customize these experiments, principles, and practices to your teams and organizations, the more effective and inspiring they will be to everyone involved.

The Responsive School Roadmap

Step	Description	Experiment	Time frame
1. Purpose	Clarify and align teams and the organization around a clear and compelling purpose.	1. Define a Clear Purpose	One hour for initial definition. Revisit on a regular basis to ensure relevance.
2. Protocols	Become fluent in agreed-on guidelines and standards.	4. Team Meeting Protocol 8. Three Language Shifts for Decision-Making Discussions 9. Protocol for a Starting Proposal	Two to four months with weekly or biweekly practice. A steady cadence and maximum participation are key.
3. Data	Solicit and share information effectively.	2. Delineate Between What You Know and What You Anticipate 3. Offer Feedback as Data 6. The One-Question Technique 7. Guidelines for Being an Effective Sensor 11. Say "Thank You" for Asking 12. The 3 × 3 Rule	Daily or weekly practice and continuous improvement.
4. Mindsets and habits	Deepen commitment and solidify a responsive culture.	10. Default to Yes and Defend No 13. Start a Reflection Practice 14. Create a Habit of Learning Every Day	Daily or weekly practice and continuous improvement.
5. Systems practices	Revisit, question, and revise organizational systems.	5. Role Mapping 15. Personal Portfolios	Four hours quarterly or semi-annually.

Step 1: Purpose—Clarify and align teams and the organization around a clear and compelling purpose.

Time frame

> One hour for initial definition. Revisit on a regular basis to ensure relevance.

Experiment

> 1. Define a Clear Purpose (page 29)

Every team or organization needs a clear and compelling purpose that functions as a North Star to guide its work. In responsive organizations the role of planning is about articulating a purpose and the vision for how to achieve it, which then helps define and align teams and roles.

Step 2: Protocols—Become fluent in agreed-on guidelines and standards.

Time frame

> Two to four months with weekly or biweekly practice. A steady cadence and maximum participation are key.

Experiment

> 4. Team Meeting Protocol (page 60)
> 8. Three Language Shifts for Decision-Making Discussions (page 114)
> 9. Protocol for a Starting Proposal (page 115)

The protocols in Chapters 2 and 4 help individuals come together to work more effectively and responsively in connected units. Think of these protocols as the rules of a board game. They are the guidelines everyone agrees to follow to ensure shared standards and effective meetings and processes. As you adopt and practice these protocols, you will surface valuable tensions and begin to shift collective habits.

Step 3: Data—Solicit and share information effectively.

Time frame

> Daily or weekly practice and continuous improvement.

Experiment

2. Delineate Between What You Know and What You Anticipate (page 31)

3. Offer Feedback as Data (page 59)

6. The One-Question Technique (page 89)

7. Guidelines for Being an Effective Sensor (page 90)

11. Say "Thank You" for Asking (page 140)

12. The 3 × 3 Rule (page 141)

Effective communication means data and information are shared in ways that are well understood, trusted, and meaningful. Chapters 1–3 all refer to the importance of data, and Chapter 5 talks about how to make information available and transparent. In all these contexts, data are critical. We need to broaden our view of data as all the information—hard and soft, experiential, anecdotal, and quantifiable—that we gather as human sensors. We need to be able to discern between data and assumptions. Finally, we need to realize that data need to be shared in ways that are useful to others.

Step 4: Mindsets and Habits—Deepen commitment and solidify a responsive culture.

Time frame

Daily or weekly practice and continuous improvement.

Experiment

10. Default to Yes and Defend No—One Decision at a Time (page 117)

13. Start a Reflection Practice (page 163)

14. Create a Habit of Learning Every Day (page 166)

The transition from discrete protocols and actions to a broader embrace of responsiveness is about embedding new habits and mindsets and then spreading them intentionally throughout the organization. Challenging as it may be at first, we can default to yes—and catch ourselves saying no—starting with small proposals and successes that build confidence. We can reflect on and share our own goals and growth, and we can ask for advice. And we can engage in learning with the support of a peer or a community of colleagues.

Step 5: Systems Practices—Revisit, question, and revise organizational systems.

Time frame

Four hours quarterly or semi-annually.

Experiment

5. Role Mapping (page 85)

15. Personal Portfolios (page 167)

At this point in the journey of responsive individuals and organizations, we know we need to embrace change, growth, and failure. Once we gain experience, we can make a greater commitment by aligning our organization's systems, like performance reviews and the organization chart. We can look at roles across teams, including ways roles are added, dropped, and evolved. As you roll out the steps outlined here to more teams and a larger part of the organization, revisiting roles on a regular basis and thinking proactively about professional development can contribute to an organization that is more alive, motivated, and growing.

FREQUENTLY ASKED QUESTIONS AND ANSWERS

In our work around the country and in our own organizations, we hear many questions about the new organizational practices we've presented in *The NEW School Rules*, including the emotional ones about people's fears and uncertainty. We hope our responses to the most common questions will give you additional reassurance, encouragement, and hands-on guidance as you move forward with your school, teams, and organizations. If you use the mantras of the new rules and lessons (listed on pages 182–183) and the experiments we suggest (listed on pages 183–184), you'll fail safely and you'll enhance your own sense of purpose along with the responsiveness and effectiveness of your classrooms, schools, and community engagement.

Do these rules and principles really work? Do small changes make a difference?

Imagine this: you join a project team where everyone is asked to provide a reflection at the close of the meeting versus a meeting that gets cut short and everyone abruptly leaves. What would the differences feel like?

This is the kind of small change that is implemented at some very successful organizations where anyone who visits can feel the positive energy. So yes, in addition to the school and district case studies shared in this book, companies like Zappos, Valve, Spotify, and MorningStar all have integrated principles of responsiveness into their companies with strong results. It's no surprise that more agile, self-organized companies are more productive and ultimately more successful.

Can we do it on our own? Do we need to wait until we hire consultants?

Anyone can become more responsive on an individual and team basis, without outside experts. We suggest you start small with one or two experiments at a time. Once you get fluent with one or two skills, then add another. Think about it like learning how to play a piece of music. First you start with practicing a few bars. You might get stuck on a few chords that you have to practice over and over again until you can get through it with fluency. Then you go to the next set of bars.

If you want to infuse responsiveness in your team or organization more quickly or across a larger group, it certainly helps having a consultant. An effective advisor or coach can provide you with more synthesized feedback about what's working and where the snags are so you can make faster improvements. Consultants are also skilled as neutral facilitators who can help teams build trust, hold everyone to new standards and protocols, and offer coaching and feedback without favoritism or their own opinion about the work getting in the way.

You will be introduced to tools and activities customized to your situation, which speeds the learning process. But similar to learning music, you still have to practice your etudes between sessions.

Do we have to follow these "rules" word for word?

Though we've called these rules, we use that term in the broadest sense. The rule "Do unto others as you'd like them to do unto you" has limitless variations in how it is applied in real-life situations.

These rules are guideposts. As we advise in Chapter 1, you should never stick to a plan for the plan's sake. Nor should you take someone else's "best practices" as the best model for you and your organization. Your success is dependent on observation, new data, and experimenting.

There is one important point to make, though. You can expect the process of becoming more responsive to be uncomfortable. If you pivot as soon as a new way of doing things becomes challenging, you will miss out on the biggest benefits. For example, when implementing the meeting protocol, at first it can feel rigid and limiting. You might balk at taking turns to speak in meetings and waiting for your turn. If you are one of the people who has no problem speaking up, it might feel silly. However, consider the person who hasn't been comfortable speaking up during meetings who may feel liberated by the structure. These quieter team members might finally feel they have a safe space to contribute. There's an added benefit, too. Practicing the protocol forces participants to pause and reflect on what is truly important to move the work forward and what might be superfluous or only self-serving commentary.

These skills are all learned over time through practice. If you abandon the practice too soon, you won't get a chance to see how it affects you personally and the whole culture. Then, using the suggested Responsive School Roadmap or a variation, you can revisit your protocols at intervals throughout the year to review and add practices that might be beneficial.

How will we know if we're doing it right?

All change is stressful—whether "good" or "bad" or in between. The changes to become more responsive will at first feel awkward, uncomfortable, and even painful. Think about changing a swimming stroke or a basketball shot. The new technique will make us feel self-conscious, unnatural, and sore the next day. It will feel challenging to push through the shifts from the old to new mentality and new practices. That means something right is happening.

To ensure everyone's commitment as the changes take root, stay focused on measuring your progress. Look at measures like employee engagement, the number of items getting processed in meetings, the cadence of planning and decision making, and other metrics you can measure over time. Bring people together to share their reflections and make meaning of the changes. All this data will give you a sense of whether you are making progress toward your goal.

Does it need to start at the top? Can these principles work at the school and classroom level?

As we've said multiple times in the book, anyone can start this change. Of course, it's convenient if you happen to be the superintendent and can lead the shift to responsive operating practices. If not, although you can't change the organization from the top down, you can catalyze the process of change from the middle out or the bottom up. Most of the experiments at the end of each chapter can be done by one individual, acting alone. Start by assessing your own behavior, using new language, clarifying roles, and modeling small changes with your team.

You can change the way people interact with you and your team by embracing clear norms, behaviors, and culture. You can model all the practices, including making mistakes, failing, and sharing information about what's working and what's not.

Once you have "proof points" from small shifts on one team or project, it becomes easier to share what you've learned more broadly and to marshal the right resources to enact change more broadly.

What about people who don't want to engage in the new practices?

At Education Elements, a gradual approach to implementing responsive practices allowed for a lot of flexibility. People were given flexibility to get as involved as they wanted. They were told they didn't have to adopt the new practices for their meetings, but if they were team stewards and in facilitated meetings they were members of, they had to follow the meeting rules. The protocols for meetings started out very simply: engage at the beginning and end of the meeting with the check-in and checkout. Over time, new skills were added and adapted to the organization. There was one other ground rule: no one could naysay when others wanted to try the new practices. If they were in someone else's meeting, they had to participate. Two situations are common and manageable: (1) There are people who are doing good work in their roles without actively participating. (2) There are people we could easily move out of authority roles if they lack the skills and desire for autonomous decision making. Today the teams know that each meeting is an opportunity to work on how we work together and to get valuable data to help them make better decisions. As an organization, we gauge how alive our company is by thinking about how often our teams come and go as new projects get spawned. We can also feel the pulse of the organization by the frequency and types of tensions and proposals being presented to the team.

How long does it take?

There is no end date for becoming a responsive organization. Instead, think about the work in terms of sprints and cycles of continuous evolution. When using the Roadmap to evolve your organization, step back in two-week, one-month, three-month, or six-month cycles. Experiment with what works for you and your stage of development and fluency. It's all about making data-driven decisions versus decisions based on a static plan.

Are you advocating a model? A movement? A process?

The approach to responsive organizations we've presented in this book can be thought of as an *operating system for responsive organizations* adapted to the work of schools and educational organizations.

The ideas we've presented in this book are based on the belief that static and rigid organizational systems no longer work. Information is traveling too fast, and the rate of change is quicker and more unpredictable than ever before. We believe organizations need to be more responsive to the changing conditions around them, and the only way that is going to happen is by focusing on teams with a clear purpose as the node of change, sharing information through network effects, and cultures of continuous evolution and learning.

Our hope is that this responsive organizational approach inspires transformation at the individual, team, and organizational levels and beyond. Embracing principles and lessons allows each of us to be a steward of responsiveness in our own roles and teams. A focus on action and experimenting can inspire us to move the conversation beyond theoretical models and musings into real, tangible steps. The application of these responsive principles can help improve and develop our schools, organizations, and the potential in all of us.

LIST OF NEW RULES AND LESSONS

Plan for Change, Not Perfection (Planning)

- Build Roadmaps, Not Manuals (page 24)
- Use Cadences and Pivot Points, Not Just Schedules and Deadlines (page 26)
- Encourage Testing, Experiments, and Responsiveness (page 27)

Build Trust and Allow Authority to Spread (Teaming)

- Clarify the Purpose of Every Team . . . and Revisit It (page 50)
- Build Trust and Address Tensions (page 52)
- Develop Team Habits That Support Distributed Authority (page 54)
- Embrace Dynamic Team Structures That Evolve and End (page 55)

Define the Work Before You Define the People (Managing Roles)

- Put a Role's Purpose Before Politics (page 79)
- Separate Roles for Personal Clarity and Smarter Decisions (page 80)
- Value Each Voice as a Human Sensor (page 83)

Aim for "Safe Enough to Try" Instead of Consensus (Decision Making)

- Get Aligned and Clear Out the Noise (page 107)
- Decide on Things You *Can* Decide On: Make Decisions Smaller (page 109)
- Fail Forward: Approach Planning and Big Decisions as Decision Cycles (page 111)

Harness the Flow and Let Information Go (Sharing Information)

- Accept Ambiguity (page 133)
- Think of Others: Apply the Reverse Precautionary Principle (page 136)
- Ask for What You Need: Apply the Lesson of Self-Advocacy (page 138)
- Plan Communication as a Process, Not an Event (page 139)

Schools Grow When People Grow (The Learning Organization)

- Use the Physical Environment to Build a Learning Environment (page 156)
- Promote Optimal Zones of Learning (for Adults as Well, Not Just Kids) (page 157)
- Develop a Learning Mindset: The Stance of Agent, Not Subject (page 159)
- Face the Truth (page 161)

LIST OF EXPERIMENTS

Planning

1. Define a Clear Purpose (page 29)
2. Delineate Between What You Know and What You Anticipate (page 31)

Teaming

3. Offer Feedback as Data (page 59)
4. Team Meeting Protocol (page 60)

Managing Roles

5. Role Mapping (page 85)
6. The One-Question Technique (page 89)
7. Guidelines for Being an Effective Sensor (page 90)

Decision-Making

8. Three Language Shifts for Decision-Making Discussions (page 114)
9. Protocol for a Starting Proposal (page 115)

online
resources

Visit **www.newschoolrules.com** for additional resources and tools created by Keara Duggan.

References

Anderson, M. K. (2013). *Tending the wild.* Berkeley, CA: University of California Press.

Bernstein, E., & Nohria, N. (1991, February). Note on organizational structure. *Harvard Business School Background Note* (491–083). (Revised May 2016)

Bezos, J. P. (2017). 2016 letter to shareholders. Retrieved from https://www.amazon.com/p/feature/z6o9g6sysxur57t

Bloom, B. (1984). The 2 sigma problem: The search for methods of group instruction as effective as one-to-one tutoring. *Educational Researcher, 13*(6), 4–16. Retrieved from http://web.mit.edu/5.95/readings/bloom-two-sigma.pdf

Davidson, A. (2015, May 5). What Hollywood can teach us about the future of work. *New York Times Magazine.*

Di Carlo, M. (2015, January 22). Update on teacher turnover in the U.S. Retrieved from http://www.shankerinstitute.org/blog/update-teacher-turnover-us

Estimate the cost of a meeting with this calculator. (2016, January 11). *Harvard Business Review.* Retrieved from https://hbr.org/

Fried, K. (2013, October 16). 21 reasons to quit your job and become a teacher. *Huffington Post.* Retrieved from https://www.huffingtonpost.com/

Fullan, M. (2004). *Leading in a culture of change.* San Francisco, CA: Jossey Bass.

Gino, F., & Staats, B. (2015, November). Why organizations don't learn. *Harvard Business Review.* Retrieved from https://hbr.org/

Greenfield, R. (2015, March 30). Zappos CEO Tony Hsieh: Adopt Holacracy or leave. *Fast Company.* Retrieved from https://www.fastcompany.com/

Gupta, ManMohan. (2016, May 9). Nokia CEO ended his speech saying this "we didn't do anything wrong, but somehow, we lost." Retrieved from https://www.linkedin.com/pulse/nokia-ceo-ended-his-speech-saying-we-didnt-do-anything-manmohan-gupta/

Hamel, G. (2011, December). First, let's fire all the managers. *Harvard Business Review*. Retrieved from https://hbr.org/

Hanson, S. (2012, November 9). How Zara grew into the world's largest fashion retailer. *New York Times*. Retrieved from http://www.nytimes.com

Hattie, J. (2012). *Visible learning for teachers: Maximizing impact on learning*. New York, NY: Routledge.

Kalb, C. (2014, July 21). How a team of doctors at one hospital boosted hand washing, cut infections and created a culture of safety. *Yahoo News*. Retrieved from https://www.yahoo.com/news/

Known knowns, known unknowns and unknown unknowns: A retrospective. (2006, November 9). *CBS News*. Retrieved from https://www.cbsnews.com

Laloux, F. (2014). *Reinventing organizations*. Brussels, Belgium: Nelson Parker.

Lang, S. S. (2006, December 22). Mindless autopilot drives people to dramatically underestimate how many daily food decisions they make, Cornell study finds. *Cornell Chronicle*.

Lew, C. (2017, March 7). Unlock honest feedback with this one word. *Signal v. Noise*. Retrieved from https://m.signalvnoise.com

McChrystal, S. (2015). *Team of teams*. New York, NY: Penguin.

McLeod, S. (2012). Zone of proximal development. Retrieved from http://www.simplypsychology.org/Zone-of-Proximal-Development.html

Meadows, D. H. (2008). *Thinking in systems*. White River Junction, VT: Chelsea Green.

MindShift. (2014, December 3). What meaningful reflection on student work can do for learning. Retrieved from https://ww2.kqed.org/

Newberg, A., & Waldman, M. R. (2012). *Words can change your brain*. New York, NY: Hudson Street Press.

PBS. (2004, November 16). Is Wal-Mart Good for America? *Frontline*.

RadiumOne. (n.d.). *Drugs, data and tech: Has marketing utopia arrived?* Retrieved from https://www.marketingonline.nl/sites/default/files/RadiumOne_Research_Drugs_Data_Tech.pdf

Responsive.org. (n.d.). Manifesto. Retrieved from http://www.responsive.org/manifesto

Ries, E. (2011). *The lean startup*. New York, NY: Crown Business.

Robertson, B. J. (2015). *Holacracy: The new management system for a rapidly changing world*. New York, NY: Henry Holt.

Rozovsky, R. (2015, November 17). The five keys to a successful Google team. Retrieved from https://rework.withgoogle.com/blog/five-keys-to-a-successful-google-team/

Science and Environmental Health Network. (2017). Precautionary principle, understanding science in regulation. Retrieved from http://sehn.org/precautionary-principle/

Sinek, S. (2009). *Start with why: How great leaders inspire everyone to take action*. New York, NY: Penguin.

Spillane, J. P. (2006). *Distributed leadership*. San Francisco, CA: Jossey Bass.

Strang, D., & Macy, M. W. (2001). In search of excellence: Fads, success stories, and adaptive emulation. *American Journal of Sociology, 107*(1), 147–182.

Suzuki, S. (1970). *Zen mind, beginner's mind*. Trumble, CT: Weatherhill.

Zuieback, S. (2012). *Leadership practices for challenging times: Principles, skills and processes that work*. Ukiah, CA: Synectics.

Index

A SAGE Publishing Company

Helping educators make the greatest impact

CORWIN HAS ONE MISSION: to enhance education through intentional professional learning.

We build long-term relationships with our authors, educators, clients, and associations who partner with us to develop and continuously improve the best evidence-based practices that establish and support lifelong learning.